Preparing *for* Childbirth

Preparing for Childbirth

Relaxing for Labor ✦ Learning for Life

Betty Parsons, M.B.E.

FISHER
BOOKS™

Publishers	Bill Fisher
	Helen Fisher
	Howard Fisher
Managing Editor	Sarah Trotta
Production	Casa Cold Type, Inc.
Cover Photo	PhotoDisc™
Cover Design	Fifthstreet Design
Illustrations	Jane Fallows
Cartoons	Bill Piggins

Published by:
Fisher Books
4239 W. Ina Road, Suite 101
Tucson, AZ 85741
(520) 744-6110

Copyright © 1996, 1997 by Betty Parsons.
First published 1996 by Aurum Press Limited, London, England

The right of Betty Parsons to be identified as Author of this work has been asserted by her in accordance with the Copyright, Design and Patents Act 1988.

Printed in U.S.A.
Printing 10 9 8 7 6 5 4 3 2 1

Library of Congress Cataloging-in-Publication Data
Parsons, Betty, 1917—
    [Understanding childbirth]
    Preparing for childbirth : relaxing for labor, learning for life / Betty Parsons.
        p.   cm.
    Previously published under the British title: Understanding childbirth.
    ISBN 1-55561-128-1
    1. Pregnancy.   2. Childbirth.   I. Title.
RG525.P256   1997
618.2′4—dc21   618.24   97-7177
                                       Pars   CIP

For Zoë and Harriet, with love

Acknowledgments

The gestation period of this book has been a long one. I want to thank the many expectant mothers and fathers who, over the years, have by their consistent pressure and encouragement helped in its production. I also want to thank my literary agent, Charlotte Howard, and my publisher, Sheila Murphy, for their continued enthusiasm and help. To Lizzie Hibbitt, RGN, RM, my heartfelt thanks for always being there to answer my questions on changing obstetrical procedures.

Especially I want to thank Elspeth Arden, who rescued me from my inability to understand modern technology, took my typescript and transferred it to a computer. Her many hours of practical assistance, her advice and encouragement helped immeasurably in the safe delivery of this baby.

Contents

Introduction

Many people have asked me what "method" of preparation for childbirth I use. I have never taught any particular method. I do not believe in building up a woman's expectations to the point where she is looking for a wonderful experience where nothing can interfere with her goals. Labor is not easy and it does not necessarily fulfill a woman's dreams. It does not always go according to plan. Situations beyond anyone's control may arise that demand the need for expert obstetrical skill. Women who approach their confinements with particularly high expectations can be greatly traumatized by the reality of the situation.

As time passed during the early years of my prenatal teaching, I began to realize that preparing women for labor was not sufficient. Pregnancy and labor are not events separate from the rest of life. They are part of the whole. Having a baby does not stop with the moment of birth. It is the start of motherhood and fatherhood, bringing all the joys and problems inherent in these new roles. All parents will agree, I am sure, that parenthood is one of the most difficult jobs in life.

With this in mind, I started to stress the need to learn the art of relaxation, which is more than just relaxing one's body and doing nothing. It is a way of life. It is learning to live one day at a time, doing one thing at a time. It is learning to accept what we cannot change, to drop shoulders and breathe in moments of crisis and difficulty. I am confident that if, during her pregnancy, you can help a woman to build these strengths in herself, they will sustain her, not only in labor, but for the rest of her life.

What gives me most pleasure is when one of my "mums" or one of my "babies" who has herself become a mother tells me, "It all helped so much during labor, but it has helped even more for life." "Learning to 'drop shoulders' and to do one thing at a time has changed my life for me."

I hope that this book may help expectant mothers and fathers, not only with pregnancy and labor, but with life in general.

~ 1 ~

First Steps

You are pregnant! I wonder how you felt when you first discovered that the test was positive. Excited; happy; shocked; apprehensive; unbelieving? So many different emotions can overwhelm us when we hear the momentous news that is going to change our lives. Whatever they may be, they will fluctuate widely during pregnancy. One day you may experience a sense of euphoria and the next you may wake up feeling negative about the whole business of having a baby.

During my classes I would always ask the question, "How many of you have changed your minds about having the baby?" Invariably a number of hands shot up. I remember one mother-to-be who put both arms up into the air! I remember too the look of relief on each woman's face as she realized that she was not alone in her times of doubt and depression. It is always comforting to know that one is normal.

Mood Swings and Hormone Changes

It is important to understand the reasons for these mood swings. As soon as you become pregnant, hormone changes start to occur in the body and continue throughout pregnancy. Hormones play an extremely important part in how we feel and react to circumstances They can make us feel happy or depressed, energetic or sluggish, fearful or optimistic, angry or loving. There is nothing you can do to alter these mood swings but it helps to accept them and to know that the negative ones, which can be so distressing, will pass.

I have known thousands of pregnant women who have felt very guilty when they burst into tears for no apparent reason, or became angry about something trivial. It is usually the one who is nearest and dearest who is the butt of your tears or irritability, so it helps if he too understands that hormonal activity beyond your control is responsible for the mood swings.

Over the years many expectant mothers have said to me: "I'm being awful to him and I feel so guilty;" "I feel as though my character has changed. Will I ever be myself again?"; "If anyone is kind to me, I cry, and if someone is slightly critical, I cry. I just seem to cry over anything." I can reassure anyone who has these problems that, given a little time following the birth of her baby, when hormonal activity returns to normal, she will return to her prepregnant normal self.

Losing Your Memory and Focus

Another problem a woman can have during pregnancy is not being able to focus. She can forget what day it is, what time it is, or what she was supposed to be doing. There are countless examples of this lack of focus and loss of memory, which can cause embarrassment. One woman drove five miles before she realized that she was going in the wrong direction. Another put a chicken to be cooked into the bathroom cupboard and the toilet paper into the refrigerator, and another put her husband's dirty socks into her briefcase prior to going to work. She was really surprised when she opened her briefcase at the office!

Yet another prepared a special casserole for guests coming to dinner, put it in the oven and forgot to turn on the oven! Her husband was very irritated because he had to take the guests out to dinner. "Don't blame me," she told him, "blame my hormones." Luckily he had a good sense of humor so all was forgiven. And you need a sense of humor to cope with the problems that these hormonal changes can bring.

It is difficult when relatives and friends expect you to be glowing with happy anticipation at every moment. But when the dark days come and you wonder why you ever embarked on parenthood, it is comforting to understand the reason for the mood swings. Do not feel guilty. Try to accept them. They will pass. And if you can laugh with someone about your sometimes extraordinary behavior, it will help to relieve the tensions.

Here I must reassure anyone who suffers no emotional changes. An expectant mother once said to me, "I am beginning to think I must be abnormal. I haven't had any changes at all. I've never felt sick or irritable or tearful. I am as I've always been and have felt wonderful." "Be very grateful," I said to her. "Most of us, from time to time, have the problems I've talked about, but some women are lucky. They have no problems at all, and, like you, feel very good throughout pregnancy, so be happy and enjoy every minute of it."

Anxieties and Worry are Normal

Whatever emotions may or may not be experienced, I doubt if any woman goes through her pregnancy without certain anxieties, the most common one being whether the baby will be healthy and normal. It is a natural anxiety and as the expected date of delivery grows closer it often increases. It's not until the baby has been delivered and been pronounced beautiful and healthy that the little nagging fear is totally eliminated.

Regarding this, it is worth stating that it is wrong and very stupid to tell anyone to stop worrying or not to be frightened. We can never just turn off our emotions just because we'd like to. The more we try to conceal our fears, the greater they become. We need to relax, drop shoulders and breathe. Then we can accept our fears and worries, and by accepting them, although they may not be eliminated, they will be lessened and put into proper perspective.

I once spoke to a medical audience on the subject of relaxation. I told the doctors there how irritated it made me when patients with cardiac and blood-pressure problems came to me and said,

"My doctor says I have to stop worrying so much . . . that it's my worry and anxiety that's making me worse." The patient will go away worrying about worrying, which is a double negative and will only increase the tension. After my talk, a doctor came up to see me and said, "Thank you. We come out with these clichés without thinking about the effect they can have."

There are few, if any, pregnant women whose anxieties about labor and the well-being of the baby do not increase as their expected delivery date draws nearer. Friends and relatives are apt to insist that you not worry, that everything is going to be all right. Such exhortations are not helpful, because you feel the butterflies inside you fluttering more and more as the great day approaches.

One of my "mums," who had well-meaning words to that effect said to her, replied, "Please stop telling me not to worry. I *am* worried and I am sure I will be until after the baby is born and I know that everything is all right. Your talking to me like that really doesn't help at all." That silenced the well-meaning friend. I hope it taught her to choose her words more carefully in the future.

Perhaps this habit of telling people "not to worry" persists because as children we're so used to being told not to be afraid. Adults are apt to tell children "you're a big boy (or girl)—don't be frightened." But children, like all human beings, do feel fear. If they are continuously told not to be afraid, they will grow up believing that being frightened is a sign of weakness. They will be unwilling to express their feelings for fear of being ridiculed. This will only lead to inner confusion and a damaged self-image, which can cause great problems as the years pass.

No Shame in Being Afraid

Better by far to explain to a child that there is no shame in being afraid, and with understanding encourage him or her to discuss the situation. A child who grows up knowing that whatever emotions or difficulties he may experience can be discussed without destructive criticism will become a much happier and more relaxed adult. And an adult who is willing to admit to being afraid is well on the way to accepting the situation and thus bringing it under control.

Pregnant women are both vulnerable and suggestible and can be greatly affected by thoughtless remarks, especially if they are from people who delight in dramatizing their own labors. I have known many who have been worried by comments about the possible size of the baby. The long-waisted can be made to think that her baby is too small, and the short-waisted given the idea of a big baby that she may have difficulty delivering. I remember one tall, long-waisted woman whose pregnancy was hardly noticeable right up to her delivery date. She had an 8-pound daughter!

In the same class was a woman just five feet tall and short-waisted. She did indeed look as though she might have twins or a very big baby. She delivered a 6-pound baby without any difficulty. Both had worried silently from remarks such as, "Are you sure your baby is all right? You look very small to me." "Goodness. You have a big baby in there. I hope it won't be too difficult for you." The tall, long-waisted woman will never show her pregnancy as much as the short-waisted. It is the latter who has to suffer more discomfort during the later part of her pregnancy.

It is difficult not to be affected by what people say and tell you, but it is important not to keep your worries bottled up inside. Don't feel guilty about them. You are a normal pregnant woman, subject to all the little worries and anxieties that affect us all from time to time. Remember the saying, "A trouble shared is a trouble halved." Never be afraid to express your anxieties. Discuss your worries with the professionals who are caring for you. Ask your questions and so receive the answers that will put your mind at rest.

Fatigue and Rest

As pregnancy progresses, fatigue will increase. It is inevitable. I have never known a woman who has not felt very tired during the last few months of pregnancy. You must accept it, give into it and REST without any sense of guilt or laziness. During the last two months of pregnancy, the baby is doubling his or her weight. The weight gain puts an extra strain on your body and on your movements. Most women find it more difficult to move around and to find a comfortable position during the last two months, especially those who are short-waisted.

It is essential that you do not become overtired to the point of exhaustion. This is not good for you, not good for the baby and not good for your relationships. We all know the effect of being physically overtired. It affects every aspect of our lives. We do not cope with life as efficiently as we would wish. Our spirits droop and often a sense of failure and dejection creeps in. Minor irritations assume unrealistic proportions. Molehills become mountains, and we find ourselves reacting angrily to some well-meant humorous remark. After a good rest we find the sun has come out, the black clouds have disappeared, and we can laugh again and look more positively at life.

The baby depends on you: REST!

Always remember that your baby receives his or her vital life-giving oxygen and nutrition through your body and blood supply. So for the sake of your baby, yourself, your partner, your work, your family, your whole life, be sensible and prevent over-tiredness (which can be damaging to your health) by resting. Especially during the last two months it is important to REST EVERY DAY. Fatigue always diminishes our capabilities and lowers the pain threshold. Labor needs all one's strength and is *not* painless. You will not give yourself a proper chance for labor or for the postnatal period if you go into labor with your energy account overdrawn.

Once you are into the last two months, if life allows you to do so, go to bed every day for at least an hour. If you can make it one-and-a-half or two hours, so much the better. Relax and recharge the batteries. I promise that not only will you and your baby benefit but, when your partner comes home, he will be greeted with a smile instead of a frown, drooped shoulders and an "Oh dear! I'm so tired," which is never helpful to a good relationship. And if *he* comes home with a frown, drooped shoulders and an "I'm so tired—I've had an awful day," you will be able to handle his mood without aggravating it into an argument.

Many people have told me that they dislike resting in the afternoon because they feel groggy when they get up and find it difficult to get started again, especially if they have been to sleep. You can avoid this feeling if you set an alarm so that you don't sleep too long and don't try to get up too quickly. Give yourself a little time to wake up, think how much your baby has benefited from your rest, stretch your arms and legs, get up slowly, wash your face, have something to drink and you will feel refreshed and ready for what lies ahead. I cannot tell you how many expectant mothers have told me what a difference this attitude towards resting made to their lives.

If you are working full-time, of course it's not possible to take one or two hours to go to bed. I am a great believer in a woman continuing to work, if she wishes to do so, during her pregnancy. It's not wise for anyone, once she becomes pregnant, to sit, do nothing and cross off the dates on the calendar until the baby is due. If you do this, the nine months will begin to feel like nine years. It's important to live a busy, normal life. But keep everything in balance and be aware of the problems that overfatigue can cause so you can try to avoid them.

Increased Blood Pressure (Hypertension)

Any sign of increased blood pressure makes resting essential. I have known women who, despite having this problem, would not obey the order to rest. They kept on working too hard, not resting and so making things worse to the point where they were confined to total bed rest. This is a very foolish course to follow. More often than not they would have been spared this total restriction of movement if only they had been sensible and rested as they had been advised.

Swelling Feet and Ankles

Another fairly common problem that can occur is swelling of the feet and ankles. It is always increased by long periods of standing and during hot weather. Again, rest is all-important for this condition. Put your feet up whenever possible and try to arrange support for your legs so they are resting in an upwards position of approximately 45 degrees.

Use Your Lunch Break to Rest

If you are an expectant working mother, try always to use part of your lunchtime break to find somewhere to sit, put your feet up if possible and relax for a little while. Many women use that free hour to rush out, do a lot of shopping and end the day exhausted. It's a mistake. Also get to bed early on some nights, so you have some prolonged hours of rest. I certainly do not advocate giving up all social life. This would be depressing for both you and your partner. Do not burn the candle at both ends. Go to bed early three or four times a week.

Sleep Can Be Difficult

Very few women sleep as well as usual during the last two or three months. The baby seems to take pleasure in kicking more vigorously once you have laid down to sleep. You have to empty your bladder more frequently and it is difficult to get comfortable in bed. This interferes with your sleep pattern. But even if you are not sleeping, you will be resting and restoring your energy. By doing this you will be able to keep working without becoming exhausted, which is often the reason women stop working sooner than they had anticipated.

~ 2 ~

The Importance of Exercise

There is a lot of talk about the importance of prenatal exercises. In fact, some people imagine prenatal preparation classes to be little more than the routine performance of physical exercises, which, if done regularly, will help ensure a trouble-free, "natural" birth. Others are under the impression that if they do not do a series of exercises, it could lead to unnecessary difficulties during their pregnancy. Neither of these beliefs is true. I have known women who were so exercise-minded that they overstretched muscles, much to their detriment. Others, who for some medical reason had to forego all exercise, still had happy and fulfilling labors.

Don't Feel Guilty about Exercise

Some women dislike exercising and this can cause a great sense of guilt. They feel they are not doing the best for themselves or their babies. Guilt is a negative emotion and only causes stress and tension, which is exactly opposite from what we want for a pregnant woman. Although exercise during pregnancy is important, it should always be kept in balance and never overdone. For anyone who enjoys doing exercises, I suggest you find a good prenatal exercise class that you can attend regularly and exercise within a group, which usually makes exercising more pleasurable.

Beneficial Daily Exercise

Here are a few simple exercises that even the non-exercise-minded person will find easy to incorporate into her daily life. If done regularly, they will help keep your body in good muscular tone as well as giving you a sense of well being. First, it is important to remember that the mental attitude we bring to exercising will or will not make it beneficial. It is essential that, as you do an exercise, you *think* about what you are doing and why you are doing it. BE AWARE. If, while you are exercising, you are at the same time thinking about what you should prepare for dinner, you will be wasting 80% of the benefit.

Exercise 1 — to stimulate circulation

Stand with your feet parallel. Alternately raise and lower your heels, leaving your toes firmly on the floor. As you bend your feet, *really feel them moving*. It is surprising how stiff our feet can be. Change the weight from one foot to the other about 12 times, and do the exercise two or three times during the day. It will help stimulate the circulation in your legs and will also strengthen the leg muscles, which will help you stand and walk correctly. For anyone who has a desk job, it is good to do this a few times during the day.

Exercise 2 — for leg cramps

If you are troubled by leg cramps during the night, first do the previous exercise and then follow it with this one. Balance yourself while standing by holding onto something, and then roll a bottle under your bare foot back and forth 20 times. Do it first with one foot and then with the other.

Why this works I don't know, but many expectant mothers have told me how much it has helped when they have done it before getting into bed. With cramps, the important thing to remember is never to stretch your legs by pointing your toes. This often triggers cramps. Always, when you stretch, stretch by pulling your feet up and backward. If you should suddenly get a cramp, by doing this quickly you can usually counteract it. If not, then get your partner to press your foot very firmly backwards and to press his thumb into the calf muscle. I have known many men who have been rudely awakened to perform this expectant father's job!

Exercise 3 — for the PC muscle

This is a very important exercise. It works the pubococcygeus muscle (PC muscle) of the pelvic floor. The pelvic floor is that part of your body between your legs where three passages are located. There is the back passage (the rectum), the middle passage (the vagina, through which your baby will be born), and the front passage (the urethra, through which you urinate). The diagram below may give you a better idea. Imagine you are looking down into your pelvis from above. I want you to try to think of pulling the PC muscle up.

Stand with your feet parallel and your knees relaxed. Imagine that your bladder is full and you need to go to the bathroom, that you have a tampon in the vagina that feels as if it were coming out and that your bowels have to move. What a dilemma to be in!

There is no bathroom nearby. What are you going to do? To prevent an embarrassing situation, you need to tighten up those three passages. Imagine you are looking down into your pelvis from above and think of pulling the PC muscle *up*. It's not always easy to do at first, but with practice you will become good at it and it will pay great dividends, not only for the birth of the baby,

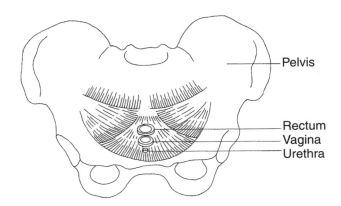

The pelvis and the pelvic floor

Any time, any place, anywhere . . .

but even more so afterward. If you learn to keep the PC muscle in good shape, you will help prevent some of the problems that can follow the birth, such as incontinence.

Do this exercise several times a day. It's better to do it three times slowly, concentrating on what you are doing, than to do it ten times without proper thought. You can do it as you go through your day. While waiting for a teapot to boil, doing the ironing, standing at the sink, take a few moments to concentrate and pull up the PC muscle. You can even do it while waiting for a bus. With practice you will find that it becomes a habit.

Exercise 4 — stretching inner thigh muscles

This exercise has both a physical and a psychological purpose. It will help stretch the inner thigh muscles. In addition it will help you become used to the idea that this is the most probable position that you will be in during the second stage of labor. That's when you will be pushing your baby down the birth canal. Many women have an ingrained dread of exposing themselves in this rather undignified position. This is an attitude we must try to change because no one, I assure you, can have her baby with her knees crossed. If this dread does exist, it can cause tension in the muscles that should be relaxed and so interfere with the progress of the second stage of labor.

Prop yourself up on pillows with your knees bent as shown in the illustration. Let your knees fall apart. Put your hands on the inside of your knees and press them outwards with gentle pushes. You will feel the inner thigh muscles stretching. Relax and repeat. Don't ever try to push your knees out with short, jerking pushes. This achieves nothing.

Do this eight or ten times a day and then, for a few moments, just lie relaxed with your legs falling apart as much as possible and think to yourself, "This is the position I may be in for the second stage of labor." If you have any apprehension about assuming this position, I promise you that, if you do this exercise every day, you will come to terms with this particular "dragon" and it will enable you to cooperate fully in the birth of your baby.

I remember one young woman whose biggest fear this was. The thought of lying exposed with unknown professionals looking at her was causing her sleepless nights. She told me that when she started doing this exercise, she blushed and felt tense, even in the privacy of her own bedroom. However, she kept at it, doing it every day, and after two weeks the fear had gone completely. She had a very happy labor.

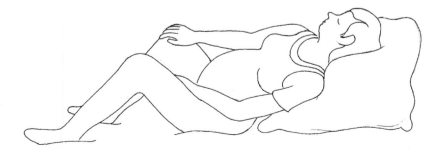

A labor-saving exercise

Sitting cross-legged is sometimes advocated as a good way to stretch the inner thigh muscles. Some women can sit cross-legged quite easily all through pregnancy, and in fact find it comfortable. Others find it difficult to do. It depends very much on a woman's stature, length of legs and size of abdomen. Remember never to force your body into a position that is uncomfortable. You can give birth to a baby without learning to sit in the lotus position!

Exercise 5 — for pectoral muscles

This exercise is for the pectoral muscles. Hold your arms as shown in the illustration below, making sure your elbows are at shoulder level. Each forearm is held above the wrist with the opposite hand. Push the skin of your arms towards the elbow without moving your hands. You should feel a tightening of the muscles on each side at the top of your chest. Repeat this eight or ten times and do it several times a day. It is wise to wear a well-fitted bra. Make sure that you change your bra size as your breasts enlarge.

Exercise 5

Exercise 6 — posture and walking

Now I come to what I consider the two most important "exercises" of all—posture and walking. By standing and walking correctly, you will be exercising certain muscles all the time, besides which, you will *feel* much better.

Posture

How do you stand? With your knees stiff and your shoulders braced back? That is wrong. If you stand like this, you can feel the top part of your body bent slightly backwards. This throws your whole body out of alignment, which can cause backache. In addition, it raises your chest, which interferes with correct breathing.

Stand with your feet parallel and your knees relaxed so that the weight of your body is forward, on the balls of your feet. I do not want you to bend your knees, but just let them give a little so they aren't stiff. When you do this, you will feel your tailbone tuck under, your back will straighten out and your abdominal muscles will automatically pull in. Now tighten your buttocks a little and let your shoulders be down and relaxed. By "down" I don't mean they should be slouched. There is a great difference between shoulders being "down" and being slouched. Let your arms hang at your sides. Hold your head straight with your neck and jaw relaxed. Think tall and feel you are standing *on* the ground rather than sinking your weight *into* it.

Now stiffen your knees, brace your shoulders back and feel the difference. Correct this position again. Do this several times so that you are really aware of the difference. This new way of standing may seem a little strange at first. But if you practice it and correct yourself when you notice you are standing wrongly, it will soon become a habit. Standing like this is an exercise in itself. Your leg muscles are carrying the weight of your body, your abdominal muscles are automatically pulled in and there is minimal strain on your back. With your shoulders relaxed you will breathe correctly and get the maximum amount of oxygen into your lungs, which will benefit not only you but also your baby. Never forget that

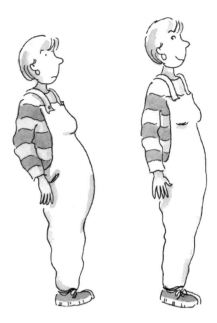

"Where's the bulge gone?"

your baby's nourishment and oxygen supply come through your body. Every expectant mother should remember this.

I remember a young woman in my class (and she certainly wasn't the only one) who was standing in what I call a "maternity slouch." Her weight was back on her heels, the upper part of her body and shoulders were tipped backwards, and her abdomen with the bulge was protruding forwards. She had a backache and at seven months looked as though she might have the baby at any moment. She felt heavy, tired and bored with her pregnancy. I showed her how to change her posture with her weight forward so she could gently bounce her heels up and down, relax her shoulders and think "tall." She found it difficult to believe the difference. The "bulge" had automatically pulled in, the strain was off her back, she was breathing easily and she could see her feet again! She looked down, felt her abdomen and said, "Where'd it go?"

Walking

To walk correctly, remember that it is your legs that have to do the work. Too often people walk with their shoulders tensed and chest lifted. This puts unnecessary strain on the back and interferes with the correct oxygen intake. Or they walk with shoulders drooped, dragging their bodies around, which is just as wrong. Think of your legs as your two donkeys and make them do the work for which they were intended. Hold your body tall, let your shoulders be relaxed but not slouched. Then, moving from your hips, try to think of walking *over* the ground, with the end of one step being the beginning of the next, rather than each step going *into* the ground.

Walk tall

Always remember that the way we stand and walk affects the way we feel. And the way we think affects the way we stand and walk. If you think "heavy," "pregnant," and "elephant," you will feel *very* heavy, VERY PREGNANT, and you will look as well as feel like an an elephant. Think "slim" and "feather," which I know sounds ridiculous. You will find that as you automatically pull in your abdominal muscles you will actually *look* slimmer and certainly feel less like an "elephant." And you will begin to carry yourself, rather than drag yourself around. It will pay you many dividends at all levels of your being. So many women whom I have taught have told me years after their babies were born how much this attitude helped them in their lives.

Thinking "feather"

Stairs

Many women find stairs a problem during the later months of pregnancy, but by walking in the way I have suggested stairs can be turned into an exercise. Instead of pulling yourself up by the banisters, stair by stair, use the banisters as a balance and then make your donkeys carry you up the stairs. Once again, the leg muscles are strengthened and the abdominal muscles are tightened. Strain on your back is minimized and, with your shoulders relaxed, your breathing is easier—all lessening the energy expenditure.

An expectant mum I once taught lived with three flights of stairs. Thinking "feather" and making her donkeys do the work changed her whole attitude. She told me, "I hated the stairs and used to drag myself up feeling very 'elephant-like' and upset. I was exhausted when I reached the top. Now I think positively. I talk to them, and say, 'Stairs, I am going to use you as my exercise,' and then I think 'feather,' put my donkeys to work and up I go. The difference is unbelievable."

Another young woman told me that she was "feathering" her way up the stairs when her partner said to her, "What are you doing?" "I'm being a feather instead of an elephant," she said. He laughed so much he nearly cried. "I don't care what he thought," she said, "It's made a lot of difference to me, and I told him that he ought to try it."

Swimming

Swimming, especially the breast stroke, is an excellent exercise. The buoyancy of the water minimizes any strain, but as with all exercising, never overdo it. If you swim in the ocean, don't swim too far from the shore in case you become tired or get a sudden cramp. For the same reasons, if you are in a pool, stay within reach of the side.

Any sport-loving expectant mother must be careful of continuing with any sport where there is a danger of falling, such as horseback riding, cycling, skiing or skating.

Reasons Not to Exercise

Bleeding—If you have any bleeding, you should stop all exercise and seek medical advice. Often there is no problem, but exercise should not be resumed until you've been checked and given the necessary clearance.

Blood Pressure—Any increase in your blood pressure means no more exercise and necessitates maximum rest.

Small Baby—If the baby shows signs of being "small for its due date," it is essential to rest as much as possible. The more you exercise, the more energy and oxygen you are using, which can adversely affect the nourishment going to the baby.

Don't Get Overtired—However much exercise you do, remember that tired muscles lose their tone, so prevent getting overtired by having the proper amount of rest. Never push your body beyond its normal limits. Overexercising can be harmful, just as being too sedentary can have ill effects. Moderation and balance are the secrets of happy and healthy living, and this rule applies to exercise like everything else.

~ 3 ~

Everyday Life

During pregnancy it is important that your diet provide an adequate amount of protein, fat, carbohydrate, iron, calcium and vitamins. These are essential, both for your baby's growth and development and for your continued good health.

Protein

Protein is contained principally in meat, fish, eggs, cheese, milk, nuts, lentils and soy beans. Vegetarians must be sure to include an adequate amount of protein because it is vital to the growth of your baby. Fats and carbohydrates are also important, but be careful about the amount you eat. Avoid fried food and restrict your intake of foods that contain a lot of sugar, such as cakes, cookies, jam, chocolate and soft drinks. Over-indulgence will not only lead to unwanted weight gain, but is apt to suppress your appetite and interfere with your consumption of the essentials.

Calcium

Calcium is needed in the formation of bones and teeth. Milk is a very good source of calcium. For anyone who likes milk I suggest you drink two glasses a day, but avoid whole milk. If you dislike milk, calcium is also present in hard cheeses and in many vegetables, and can always be supplemented by taking calcium tablets.

Or try camouflaging the taste in milk shakes or in hot chocolate. Avoid drinking unpasteurized milk or eating soft cheeses.

Lack of iron in the blood is to blame for anemia, which is not uncommon in pregnant women. Liver is probably the highest source, but not everyone likes to eat it. Egg yolks, red meat, lettuce, watercress and many cooked green vegetables—especially spinach—also contain iron. When cooking spinach, never throw away the water in which it has been cooked, which is full of iron. Add it to soups and gravies.

Gaining Weight

There are conflicting opinions about what is the correct amount of weight a woman should gain during her pregnancy. Some doctors and midwives put little restriction on the total weight gain. Others suggest it be kept to about 28 pounds. I am of the latter opinion, not necessarily from a medical point of view, but from a woman's sense of well-being during the latter part of her pregnancy. If you gain an excessive amount of weight, the last two months can be very burdensome. You will feel heavy and lethargic, movement is difficult and your self-esteem can be dealt a heavy blow. You will certainly find it difficult to think "feather" instead of "elephant"! An added advantage of watching your weight is that you will regain your figure more easily and quickly after your baby is born.

Hunger attacks

If your weight increase is due to frequent attacks of hunger, which is not unusual, here are a few tips. In the morning, scrape some carrots, wash some celery, tomatoes and apples, and put them into the refrigerator, ready to eat. Then, when a pang of hunger overcomes you, eat a carrot. Raw carrot is a good source of iron and vitamins and is not fattening. A stick of celery or an apple will satisfy the desire to eat and, again, will not add pounds. But it is important to have these handy. If not, there is a great temptation to open the cookie package and, before you know it, several cookies have been devoured and several ounces have been added to your weight.

Some expectant mothers have the opposite problem and have difficulty putting on weight. This may not affect the baby, but it is not always good for the mother. For anyone who has this problem, the secret is to eat a little, often. Never try to eat the traditional three meals a day. I have known a number of women with this difficulty who have told me, "When I look at a full plate of food, any appetite I had disappears and I can't eat it." As a result, days can go by without eating a good meal. The baby will deplete the mother's reserves and she will become very tired and lack energy. So every two or three hours throughout the day, eat something—a cheese sandwich, a piece of toast and honey, a bowl of soup, a glass of milk. And when you have your main meal, serve yourself small portions. By following this routine, many women whose weight loss was causing some concern regained the necessary weight, much to everyone's relief and pleasure.

Balanced Diet

The watchword for a healthy diet is "balanced." Eat a varied diet with plenty of fresh fruit and vegetables and always remember that you are eating for two in quality, *not* quantity.

Alcohol and Drugs

Drugs and alcohol cross the placenta and go straight to your baby. The best time to stop drinking alcohol or using illegal drugs is before you even *try* to become pregnant. **There is no safe amount of alcohol or illegal drug consumption during pregnancy.** Don't drink or take illegal drugs once you are pregnant. Using alcohol and illegal drugs during pregnancy creates serious health risks for both the pregnant woman and her unborn child. For your baby's health and well-being, abstain from all illegal drugs and alcohol while you are pregnant.

It has been suggested that drinking even a small amount of alcohol during the early weeks of pregnancy can cause abnormality in a fetus or cause miscarriage. But the majority of women are not even aware of their pregnancies for the first six to eight weeks. Some may be three or four months along before they realize they are pregnant. For those who may have been drinking alcohol, even in small amounts, there could be a lot of tension and anxiety throughout pregnancy and until after they have delivered a healthy, normal baby. There is no argument that heavy drinking during pregnancy can cause Fetal Alcohol Syndrome (FAS).

Avoid nonprescription drugs

Further, it should be noted that all drugs, even over-the-counter nonprescription drugs, homeopathic remedies or home remedies should be avoided unless they are prescribed by your healthcare provider. Many of these drugs or remedies are unsafe to use during pregnancy.

Smoking

There is conclusive evidence that smoking is harmful and should be cut out altogether. For anyone who finds it difficult to give up, just think of doing it for the sake of your baby. I remember saying to an expectant mother who smoked, "At this moment your baby is a bulge who kicks you and sometimes makes you feel uncomfortable. But once you are holding your baby in your arms and he or she has become a real little person, if someone said to you, 'For the sake of your baby's health you should stop smoking,' I feel sure you would do it." Once she really understood the harmful effect her smoking could have on her unborn child, she gave up the habit. When we have a valid reason for giving up a bad habit and truly want to do so, we can usually succeed.

Once your baby is born, don't allow any smoking in the same room with the baby. It is irresponsible to submit the baby to the ill effects of passive smoking.

Sex during Pregnancy

Unless there are medical reasons not to, sexual intercourse may continue throughout pregnancy. Penetration of the penis and the physical movements of intercourse will not harm the baby. Experimentation will find the most comfortable positions for intercourse. Lovemaking should be as gentle as possible, especially during the later months.

The hormonal changes during pregnancy can affect your sexual drive. Sometimes they increase it, with the result that your sexual enjoyment can be greatly enhanced by the sense of freedom that comes from having no worries about contraception or a possible unwanted pregnancy. This is a positive aspect of hormonal change and one to be taken advantage of.

I have known women who have suffered a loss of libido, with little desire for sexual intercourse. This can create unhappiness if you do not understand that the cause is due to something beyond your control. Once again, more often than not it is the hormonal changes affecting your sexual drive, and there is no pill or potion that will automatically restore your desire to make love. Sometimes the lack of desire for sex is due to tiredness and a general feeling of lethargy or to fear, which may even be subconscious, of harming the baby.

Many times I have been asked, "Will it ever be the same again?" "Will I ever want to make love like I used to?" The answer is "Yes." It may take a little while after the baby is born, but in time everything will return to normal.

Both partners can have problems

It should be mentioned here that it can happen that a man may feel reluctant about having intercourse. He is afraid that the sexual act may harm the baby or hurt his partner. It is important to understand that *both* partners may have a problem with sex during pregnancy.

If this problem with sex happens to either of you, remember what I said in the first chapter about accepting what we cannot change. You must drop your shoulders, relax, accept the situation and talk about it with your partner. Don't stay silent, perhaps feeling guilty about your inability to respond to his loving advances. That will only build a greater tension in you. Relationships are built on sharing. It is by sharing together, talking together, and trusting in each other's understanding, that difficulties can be resolved and loving relationships can be strengthened.

~ 4 ~

Some Problems during Pregnancy

In this chapter, I will talk about some of the most common problems during pregnancy. These physical discomforts can be inconvenient. Although many of them will clear up after a month or two, it is important to remember that they don't have to interfere with the normal flow of life. Think of them as symptoms of what is happening inside you, and you may find it easier to cope. Here are some suggestions as to how you should handle them:

Backache

Backache is very common in pregnancy, especially as the baby grows bigger and your weight increases. Bad posture always makes backache worse, so it is important to watch how you are standing. Cushions and pillows can be a pregnant woman's best friends when it comes to backache. Support your back with a cushion when you are sitting. Never be shy about carrying one with you when you go to a theater, restaurant or movie house. It is much better to enjoy an evening out with your cushion rather than suffer unnecessarily without it. A humorous occasion occurred when one of my "mums" arrived at a theater carrying her cushion in a bag. A security-minded official asked what she was carrying. "It's my cushion," she said, "I'm pregnant and my back aches if I sit too long without it." "Of course," he replied, "I remember when my wife was pregnant!"

If you lie on your back, always put pillows under your thighs. This corrects any "hollow" in your back, and allows the muscles in your back to relax. To lie in this position for a short while can provide great relief from backache. It's better not to leave pillows under your thighs for more than a couple of hours, because this could interfere with the circulation in your legs.

One very important point: If, when you are lying on your back, you should feel faint, turn right over onto your front. The faintness will pass quickly. It is caused by the baby pressing on a large blood vessel and cutting off the correct flow of blood. As soon as you turn over, the pressure from the baby is relieved and the blood flow returns to normal.

Another way to relieve backache is to get on your hands and knees for a few minutes. This takes any pressure off your back.

Nausea

Nausea or "morning sickness" can be a problem during the early weeks of pregnancy. It is not always confined to the morning. It can affect women at any time of day, sometimes lasting all day and interfering with one's social life to a depressing degree. It will usually disappear by the end of the first three months, but a few unfortunate women suffer throughout pregnancy. There is no definite answer as to what causes nausea, or why some women are so badly affected while others escape it.

Here are some helpful hints to counteract nausea:

+ Before getting out of bed, eat dry toast and drink a little milk or a cup of tea.
+ Swallow a couple of teaspoonfuls of honey.
+ Sip ginger ale.
+ Make ginger tea by steeping grated or finely chopped ginger root in boiling water, and sip it slowly. This has proved effective in many

cases of nausea, and it can also help with heartburn, which can be a great problem later in pregnancy.

✦ Several homeopathic remedies can be very helpful. It is essential before using one to consult a qualified homeopathic pharmacist to obtain the correct dosage.

✦ *Never* get out of bed too quickly and start rushing around. Give yourself time to sit up in bed, have your tea, milk, toastor honey. Then do a little deep breathing before getting up *slowly.*

Before leaving the problem of nausea, I must warn you that it can sometimes return during the last few weeks of pregnancy. Without prior warning, this can come as a great surprise and lead to worries that something is wrong.

Heartburn

Heartburn can be one of the most distressing problems during the later part of pregnancy. It is caused by the enlarged uterus pressing up against the stomach. The short-waisted person is always the one who is most affected.

I've already mentioned how helpful ginger tea can be. There are also many preparations obtainable from the pharmacist that can help. The most important things are:

✦ Never eat heavy meals
✦ Never go to bed right after eating

It is better to eat little and often than to allow yourself to become very hungry and then to satisfy your hunger by eating too much. Therein lies disaster.

Another suggestion is don't lie too flat. Sleep with extra pillows, so you are propped up a little. This will help to prevent the contents of the stomach from regurgitating into your throat.

Sciatica

It's not uncommon during the last few months of pregnancy to feel a pain in the hip, which travels down the outside of the thigh. It can sometimes become severe to the point of making walking difficult and very painful. It is due to the loosening of ligaments and the sacroiliac joint, which causes pinching of the sciatic nerve. Many people think that exercise is the best treatment and go for long walks. But this only makes the problem worse. Rest is essential.

Usually only one side is affected, so always lie on your good side and put a small pillow under your tummy. Most important, put a fairly thick pillow between your thighs. This supports the sacroiliac joint and relieves pressure on the sciatic nerve. Many women I have taught have suffered this way. I remember one who had tried to "walk it off" to the point where she could hardly move. She spent two days in bed, lying in this position, which reduced the problem so she could resume an almost-normal life.

Avoid reclining chairs. Sit on firm, upright chairs while you have this problem.

Sleepiness

During the first few months of pregnancy, some women are overcome by incredible bouts of sleepiness. They find it difficult to stay awake. They will sit down and their eyes will close involuntarily. This can be a big embarrassment, especially if you are trying to keep your pregnancy a secret. I have no answer, except to give in to it whenever possible, and, most important of all, to know it is normal.

Snoring

Over the years, many expectant mothers have told me that their partners have complained that their once-silent sleeping companions have started snoring. This is due to increased mucus secretions, which affect many mucus membranes in the body. Breathing through the nose can become more difficult and during sleep it results in snoring. Don't worry. Once pregnancy is over, silent sleep will be restored.

Stretch Marks

Nothing is guaranteed to prevent stretch marks, but it is wise to keep your skin in good condition. There is a tendency to have dry skin during pregnancy, so massage your body every day with cream or oil. Choose one containing Vitamin E and rub it in well, concentrating on your abdomen, thighs and breasts.

Maternity girdle may help

If your abdomen grows heavy, to the point where you want to put your hands under your tummy to support it, try wearing a maternity girdle. I don't suggest that you wear it all the time, but many women have found it helpful on those occasions when they have to stand for a long time or walk any great distance. It has been a particular comfort for anyone who is short-waisted or who is coping with a multiple pregnancy.

People may say that by wearing a girdle you will weaken your abdominal muscles. I don't believe this is true. A good girdle, fitted by an expert, can support the weight of your abdomen and help prevent muscles and skin from overstretching. It can also help you stand correctly with your weight properly balanced, which, as I have already explained, helps tighten up the abdominal wall. You can still do your PC muscle exercise and pull in your abdominal muscles while wearing a girdle.

I have often demonstrated how helpful a girdle can be. I have stood behind the person concerned, put my arms around her middle, and with my hands have held up the weight of her abdomen. Then I said, "Now walk!" which she did while I walked behind her, still supporting the weight. The look of relief on her face told its own story. One of my "mums" wanted me to walk behind her all the way home!

Let me repeat that it is essential that a maternity girdle be fitted properly so the extra abdominal weight is supported from underneath. Never wear a tight girdle.

Varicose Veins

Varicose veins can sometimes be a problem during pregnancy. They are due to the increased volume of blood and to the circulation becoming sluggish. This is why it's important to stimulate the circulation by doing Exercise 1 (from chapter 2) regularly and by going for a brisk walk whenever possible.

Support hose

At the first sign of protruding veins in your legs, you are wise to wear support hose. They will not cure varicose veins, but they can help prevent them from becoming worse. The other very important thing to do is put your legs up whenever possible. This helps lessen the flow of blood downward. When you are sitting, put your legs up on a fairly high stool, and whenever possible raise your legs above waist level.

Use a foam wedge

It is a good idea to arrange a sofa or divan with a firm support at one end, and then at every opportunity to lie on the sofa and put your legs up. A foam wedge is useful for this. You can get one cut to whatever size you require. The width will depend on the size of your sofa. The slope of the wedge should run from 2 to 8 or 10 inches. Leave it in place so that it is always there for you anytime you can put your legs up. Another great advantage of having such a wedge is that you can use it on your bed when you are resting.

~ 5 ~

Relaxation

Ask seven different people what relaxation means to them and you will get seven different answers. "Listening to music . . . playing a round of golf . . . going for a long walk . . . lying in a hot bath . . . fishing . . . playing tennis . . . reading a good book." These are some answers I've heard over the years from people who have come to me to learn about relaxation. These are indeed good ways to escape from the strains and stresses of a busy life and are to be encouraged. But once that period of "escape" is over, too often people go back into the commotion of life and all the tensions return.

A Way of Life

Relaxation is a way of life. It is learning how to retain the sense of relaxation those different activities give and to carry it through all the busy days ahead. How can this be achieved? First, it is important to understand a couple of points.

Every human being is made up of mind, emotion and body, and these separate parts of us interact very closely. If you are tense emotionally—perhaps nervous, frightened or angry—your body will be tense. If you are tense physically, it is difficult to be calm at the emotional level. And if body and emotions are over-tense, the mind, the creative thinking you, will no longer be in control.

How often have you said to someone who was in a high state of emotional tension, "What's the matter? What are you trying to do?" only to receive the answer, "Oh! I can't even think straight any more." And how many times have you and I suffered those moments of feeling out of control with everything on top of us? Not many people realize the importance of understanding the interaction between mind, emotion and body, and the effect that one has on the other.

Keep a Positive Energy Level

The other point is this: In reality, as human beings, we are energy-production units. We take in energy and we expend energy at the different levels of our being. Life is energy and the art of relaxation is learning how to use energy correctly and how to keep your energy level positive. And, believe me, while you are pregnant and then become a parent, it is essential, if you want to remain healthy and happy and functioning at your best, to keep your energy level positive.

How can this be achieved? Here is a little lesson in physiology. Oxygen is essential for life. The healthy functioning of every organ in our bodies is dependent on oxygen. It is taken into our lungs as we breathe and is carried through the blood supply to all the cells and organs in the body. This why correct breathing, in order to fill the lungs with oxygen, is vital for health and well-being. Every time we tense a muscle, we use oxygen. Oxygen is an essential source of energy, so if there is unnecessary tension in muscles we are wasting energy. I have seen people go through their days with shoulders tense, jaw tense, hands clenched and frowning constantly. They are completely unaware of how much precious energy they were expending quite uselessly until their energy accounts were grossly overdrawn. Then they wondered why they were feeling physically, emotionally and mentally drained.

Compare this to your bank account. If you overdraw your account, you have to put money in so your checks won't bounce. So it is with life's energy account (or level). If you overdraw your account, life will warn you. You don't function as well, you feel tired all the time, you take longer to do simple jobs, you make silly mistakes, and your memory and concentration are affected. These are all signs that your energy account is negative or overdrawn. If you pay no attention and continue to overdraw on it, then life could give you something even more serious.

As well as giving prenatal classes, I have taught many busy male executives who were suffering from heart- and blood-pressure problems. Eighty percent of those patients were people who had not heeded life's warnings. They had not allowed them-selves to stop and recharge their batteries. They kept drawing on their energy accounts until life and their bodies said, "No more." Then they were forced to stop and take stock of the situation. I am happy to say that the majority were sensible, learned how to keep their energy accounts pumped up, and lived successful and ful-filled lives.

I don't want any pregnant woman to be concerned when read-ing about the possible warning letters life can send. All those signs I have mentioned are often quite normal during pregnancy. I am talking here about *relaxation for life*. For anyone who may wonder why I do this in a book primarily about pregnancy and childbirth, I say: Having a baby does not stop with having the baby. Most of it starts there and parenthood is not easy. It is one of the most difficult jobs in life. So learn all the aspects of relaxation while you are pregnant. You can then use it during labor, and importantly, you will be able to continue to use afterwards, throughout your life. The more relaxed you are in your everyday living, the happier you will be in all your relationships, with your partner and with your children. The art of relaxation is one of the greatest weapons we can have to help us through all of life's problems.

Points to Remember

How are you going to keep your energy account positive? First you need to learn how to relax your whole body totally, bringing tension in all the muscles to a minimum, and using the minimum amount of oxygen. Then the maximum amount will be passed through your lungs into your blood supply. I have already mentioned how important it is to rest during pregnancy. It bears repeating. It is not only you who will benefit, but also your baby. When your body is at rest, your baby will benefit from the extra oxygen supply that is carried by the blood passing through the umbilical cord into the placenta and into your baby's body.

Just Relax

Before you start, it is important to think about the following points. No muscle can move without nervous stimuli. Messages *must* travel along nerve fibers before any muscle can tense or relax. Bearing this in mind, you will realize that your mental attitude before you start your relaxation routine is vitally important. If you think "negative," if you think "tense," if you think "I know I can't relax" as people do so often, messages to this effect will immediately run up and down nerve fibers, causing tension in various muscles throughout the body.

Provided there is nothing abnormal about the nervous system, everyone can relax if he or she wants to. But you have to *want* to live your life to the full and to function at your optimum level. To achieve this you need to realize the importance of keeping your energy account in the black. One patient said to me, "You'll never be able to teach me to relax. I'm a very tense person. I always have been and I know I always will be." I told her, "There is only one person who can keep you from learning, and that is you. If you really want to change, you can." Sadly, it seemed that she didn't want to. She clung to her self-image as a tense person, and there was nothing anyone could do but to let her follow her own self-destructive path to ill health.

Start with a positive attitude

So always start your relaxation with a positive attitude. Lie down and make yourself comfortable using pillows, with a sense of pleasure and achievement, knowing you are able to use this time to restore the energy you'll need for whatever work lies ahead.

For anyone who wears hard contact lenses, it's a good idea to remove them before starting a period of total relaxation. When eyes relax, they usually turn upwards and lenses can slip out of the right position.

For total relaxation, you will need a horizontal surface—a bed, the floor or a reclining chair. Sitting in an armchair will still require a certain degree of tension in the neck muscles. There are several positions for relaxing, and you need to find the one most comfortable for you. If you lie on your back, be sure to put pillows under your thighs. If you lie on your side, put a small pillow under your tummy to support the weight and put one between your thighs as well. This is especially important if you suffer from sciatica. If you have a backache, a small pillow tucked into your back in addition can be very comforting.

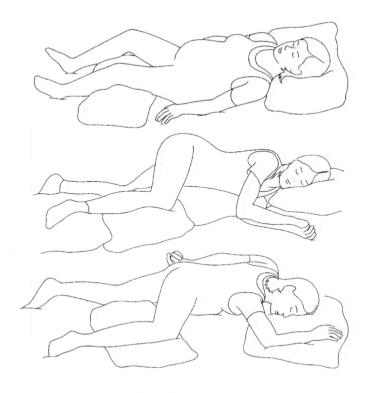

Relaxing on your back, side and tummy

"Is there any room for me?"

I've already mentioned the difficulty with sleeping that is experienced by the majority of pregnant women. If you sleep on your side, you may find that using pillows in the way I suggest greatly improves your sleeping pattern. And if you use small pillows, they won't take up much room. One of my "mums" said to me, "What will he say? There won't be any room for him in the bed." When I asked later how she had done with the pillows, she told me, "He wasn't too happy at first, but after a couple of nights, he said, 'You don't toss and turn like you did before. You're sleeping more peacefully; the pillows can stay!'"

Relaxation

Some women like lying on their tummies but are afraid this position may harm the baby. I assure you it will not cause any harm and, as long as it's comfortable, it is perfectly all right to continue to lie in this position. Just put a pillow under your tummy and one under your leg as shown on page 37.

Every human being, pregnant or not pregnant, female or male, should learn the technique of total relaxation and how to take time to "recharge." So often people think that they're wasting time and feel guilty if they stop all physical activity, lie down for a short while and "do nothing," especially when there are a thousand jobs asking for attention. To sit down or, worse still, to *lie* down, even for only 10 or 15 minutes in the midst of a busy day, is being lazy; it is failing one's duty in whatever role one is playing at that moment. Wrong!

If only more people realized that, far from being lazy and wasting time, they are using time in a very restorative and healing way. They are moving their energy levels back to a positive condition, ready to be drawn on when needed. Practicing this method of "recharging" always benefits your health, happiness, relationships and life in general.

I know from my own experience. Until I was 35, I was a rather tense person who could never allow herself a moment to escape from all the pressures of a very busy life. I was a perfectionist. Nothing must be left undone. Everything had to be done perfectly, and I was the one to do it.

Achieving a balance

Perfectionism is to be applauded, but it must be kept in balance. Balance underlies all of life. The positive and negative exist in all living things, and keeping these two aspects of life in proper balance is a secret of happy, creative living. The fear of failure, a very negative and destructive emotion, always lurks in the mind of the obsessive perfectionist, causing enormous stress and strain.

Words I read in a book many years ago helped to change my life: "For a woman to succeed, she must be willing to fail." If a person is afraid of failing, she will not even start a project. Or, having started, the inner tensions that the fear of failure provoke will prevent her from achieving the best result. Every human being fails on occasion; no one is superwoman. If we learn from our failures and accept them as another experience on the road of life, they will not have been wasted.

It is widely accepted that constant stress can undermine the body's immune system, which is the defense against infection and disease. So get your priorities straight. Learn to listen to your body and rest it when it tells you it is becoming overtired. Even a 10- or 15-minute recharge, if done with the right mental attitude, can work wonders. Always remember that prevention is better than cure.

Methods and techniques

Many books explain the art of relaxation and provide techniques for achieving this welcome state. If you will practice them regularly, you'll find it becomes easier and easier to reach a state of total relaxation.

Most techniques suggest that the first thing you do is give your body permission to "let go." By consciously—and with a sense of relief and pleasure—giving your body permission to let go, you help counteract those subconscious stimuli that have built up over the years. These may have kept your muscles under constant tension. If you have any difficulty relaxing a particular set of muscles, tense them first and then release them.

Many methods of relaxation suggest always using this technique. It can be useful, but I have known people who have become dependent on it. They cannot relax muscles unless they tense them first. I prefer people to become aware of unnecessary tensions and use their imagination and thought process to release them. But the tense/release technique is certainly useful, particularly with the shoulders and muscles across the upper part of the back, which are a common focal point of tension. As you go through your day, occasionally lift your shoulders, pull them backwards and together, and let them relax.

If you practice relaxing parts of your body in the order I suggest below, you will find it doesn't take long before you will be able to lie down, give your body permission to let go and achieve a state of total relaxation in very little time.

Permission to let go
- Hands
- Forehead, eyes and jaw
- Abdomen
- Lower back
- Legs
- Upper part of the back
- Arms

After relaxing

When you come to the end of your relaxation period, always get up *slowly*. Remember, no muscle can move without oxygen. It is only the blood that supplies the muscles with oxygen, and it is the heart and the cardiovascular system that pump the blood through the blood vessels to the muscles. So, if you jump up quickly and rush into action, the muscles cry out for oxygen and the cardiovascular system has to respond to the demand made on it. It has to work really hard. This isn't good for anyone and at least 80% of the benefit from your rest period is wasted.

As you get up, think of a cat or a dog. Except in a moment of crisis, if they have been completely relaxed, they never jump up quickly. They *always* stretch. If you watch them, you can almost feel the sense of pleasure they experience as they stretch themselves back into activity. So copy the cat or the dog. Take those few moments to stretch and come back to life.

Short relaxing periods help

If you have time for only a 15- or 20-minute "recharge," it's a good idea to set an alarm. Otherwise there is a tendency not to relax completely for fear of falling asleep and to keep looking at the clock to see if it is time to get up. So often people think that it is not worth the effort to lie down for only 15 or 20 minutes. I assure you it is! Even 10 minutes of total relaxation can work wonders for one's feeling of well-being.

Now you need to learn how to use relaxation in your every-day living. First it is important to understand that nothing can be created, no action performed, except from a point of tension. But it must be from the *correct* point of tension. A good analogy for the human being is a violin. To get a beautiful sound from that instrument the strings must be tightened. But it must be to the correct pitch. If the strings are too loose, there will be no sound. If they are too tight, they will squeak. When the tune has been played, they must be loosened. If kept too tight for too long, they will break. We need to learn how to apply the correct degree of tension and relaxation in all our different activities as we play the myriad tunes that make up the great symphony of life.

As you move through your day, try to become aware of any unnecessary tensions, those moments when the strings have been tightened needlessly. When you are sitting, relax your arms and legs. So often you see people sitting with arms tightly folded and knees crossed, legs twisted around one another. I am not against crossing your knees, but let your legs be relaxed when you do it. Arms and legs play no part in the function of sitting. Use any moments when you are sitting down, wherever it may be, as an opportunity for a mini "recharge."

Jaw can be a clue

Watch your jaw. You may be surprised to find how often it is tense. Many women I've taught have told me they had no idea how often their hands were clenched or how much they were frowning until they started to watch for needless tensions. One said that several people had remarked on the difference in her: "You look ten years younger now that you're not always frowning."

Remember that none of the tension could occur without nervous stimuli. What happens is that over the years messages from the brain are repeated so frequently that they reach a subconscious level where people are quite unaware of them. To change the subconscious messages, all you have to do is recognize any needless tension and send the message to relax. With time and practice, your awareness will become more acute and every "let go" message you send will gradually alter the subconscious stimuli—until relaxing all unnecessary muscular tension becomes a habit.

How to Deal with Emotional Tension

Do you know what I mean by a "tizzy"? My dictionary defines it as "a nervous, excited, indecisive or distracted state." We all experience tizzies from time to time, those moments when one feels overwrought and out of control. They are always a sign of emotional tension. How are you to deal with them? If you look at what you are doing when you are in a tizzy, you will always find that you're trying to change something you *cannot* change. You are saying to yourself something is not that *is,* and you can never change what "is" at any particular moment in time. It is against the law of life. **You can never do something about a situation until you accept within yourself that the situation exists.**

Here are a few examples of tizzies you will recognize. You may find yourself thinking, "I am *not* in this traffic jam," "It *can't* be as late as it is," "There *must* be a bus or a taxi coming," "The milk *hasn't* boiled over onto the freshly cleaned stove," "The saucepan *hasn't* boiled dry," "The sink *hasn't* overflowed and flooded the kitchen floor." But you *are* in a traffic jam. It *is* as late as it is. There *isn't* a bus or a taxi coming. The milk *has* boiled over. The saucepan *has* boiled dry. The kitchen floor *is* flooded. There are innumerable situations that cause tizzies.

Drop your shoulders and breathe

How can you deal with a tizzy? The first thing to do is to drop your shoulders. I guarantee that they will be tense and somewhere up around your ears! You will always find that, if you are becoming upset, your shoulders will become tense. This interferes with your breathing, which increases the emotional tension, which in turn increases the physical tension. And the spiral continues—until you feel out of control. So first relax your shoulders, then breathe out gently to the end of your breath, pause for a moment and then let your breath come in.

Never try to take in a deep breath. Just allow your breath to come in naturally. Immediately you will feel calmer and more in control. You will be able to accept the situation. It doesn't mean that you will like it. I am sure you won't, but by accepting it for what it is, you will be able to confront it and see what can be done about it.

Many women who have been to my classes have taught their children (and partners) about dropping shoulders. Once, one arrived at a refresher class and told me how she had been in a terrible tizzy, rushing around trying to get ready to come to class. Suddenly she heard her 6-year-old son say in a rather tired voice, "Oh Mommy, *please* drop your shoulders." "I burst out laughing. Talk about 'out of the mouths of babes.' I dropped my shoulders, breathed a couple of times and calm was restored."

Another of my "mums" once said to me, "Dropping shoulders is as good as taking a tranquilizer." "It's much *better*," I told her, "You carry it within you, it works instantly and has no nasty side effects."

So let "drop shoulders" be a watchword for life. As you practice this, you will find it easier and easier to do until it becomes the subconscious response to those moments of crisis.

Only One Thing at a Time

A great truth of life is that we have only one day to live at a time—today. And during today we have only one moment to live, which is now, and in that "now" there is only one thing we can do at a time. There is nothing more tiring or guaranteed to cause tizzies than to go rushing around trying to do six things at once. It is soul-destroying to have half-finished jobs staring at you, demanding attention. For anyone who goes through the day like this, here is how you can change this habit.

If you find yourself going from one unfinished job to the next, just stop. Say to your body *"Stop,"* and it will stop. Then drop your shoulders. They are sure to be tense. Breathe out. Let your breath come in and say to yourself (I believe in talking out loud to yourself because then you have to listen): "Finish this one job before you go to the next," and make yourself do it. When it is finished, either mentally or literally check it off and go on to the next thing to be done. You will be amazed to find how much more can be accomplished with a minimum of effort. As with everything, you'll need to practice, but it is practice that you will never regret.

I remember so well one of my expectant "mums" who told me about the evening she had friends over for dinner. It had been a busy day. She came home from work to find a few unexpected problems and then started rushing around to prepare the meal. "I found myself leaving the potatoes half-peeled while I looked to see if I had onions. Then I started doing something else, so the potatoes were still left half-peeled. I was getting myself into a real tizzy and remembered what you'd said. I said out loud '*Stop,* drop your shoulders and finish this one job before you start the next one.' It was unbelievable how well it worked. Everything got done and I had time to change and welcome our friends feeling quite calm."

The busier a person is, the more important it is to practice doing one thing at a time. It is integral to the art of relaxation.

When, in my classes, I talked about tizzies and learning how to do one thing at a time, I found many questioning expressions directed at me, as if to say, "Why are you talking about these things? They have nothing to do with childbirth. We only came here to learn about labor and having a baby." Having a baby is part of life. They can never be separated. The truths that apply to one must apply to the other.

Accepting Labor and Life

There are two certainties of labor. The first is that there is no blueprint. No one can prophesy what your labor will be like or what pattern it will follow. You cannot change your own pattern of labor. You have to try to accept it as it progresses. I have taught many women who, for some obstetrical reason, needed the help of a forceps or vacuum-assisted delivery, or unexpectedly had to undergo a Cesarean section. They told me afterwards that those words "Accept your own pattern of labor" helped them remain as relaxed as possible in what were sometimes difficult circumstances.

The second certainty, so vital for anyone in labor, is to remember that there is only *one* contraction to deal with at a time. As you go through your everyday life, practice dropping your shoulders and accept what you cannot change. Deal with tizzies and doing one thing at a time. You will soon find that, when you arrive at that part of life called *labor,* you will be far more able to accept your own pattern. And you will be able to accept each contraction as it starts and breathe with the contractions *one at a time.*

Just as important, perhaps even more important, is that these phrases can become the touchstones that will be the guidelines for the rest of your life.

~ 6 ~

The First Stage of Labor

Now we come to labor itself. There are three stages:

- ✦ The first stage lasts from the start of labor until full dilation of the cervix has taken place. This is nearly always the longest part of labor.
- ✦ The second stage is when the baby is ready to be delivered and when you will be asked to push the baby out.
- ✦ The third stage is the expulsion of the placenta, the afterbirth.

Before I explain how breathing and relaxation techniques relate to labor, it's important to understand the muscle action of the uterus. The uterus—the womb—is a pear-shaped organ in the pelvic cavity. Its muscular makeup is complex but it isn't necessary to understand it in detail. To get a picture in your mind of what is happening during labor, look at the diagram of the uterus at full term on page 48; that is, when you have reached your Estimated Date of Delivery (EDD).

The lines indicate two sets of muscles. The longitudinal muscles go up and over the body of the uterus, and during pregnancy they allow the uterus to stretch and enlarge to accommodate the growing baby. The horizontal, circular muscles concentrated around the lower segment of the uterus are contracted to keep the cervix closed.

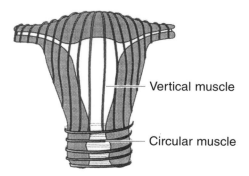

Vertical muscle

Circular muscle

The uterus at full term

Think of the cervix as the door that is kept closed during pregnancy to keep the baby safely in the uterus. There he or she can grow, develop and come to maturity to the point when it will be perfectly safe to be born. But before the baby *can* be delivered, the cervix has to be dilated; the door has to be opened to let the baby out. This is what the contractions, the so-called *pains of labor,* are doing.

When you go into labor, the long muscles start rhythmical contractions which, one by one, are pulling up and retracting the circular muscles and dilating the cervix. Little by little, each one opens the door farther until the cervix is fully dilated and it becomes possible for your baby to be delivered.

Every Contraction is a Positive Event

Understanding the purpose of the contractions can alter your whole attitude towards labor. It changes the negative to the positive. A contraction will no longer be just a pain that is happening to you. It becomes a positive, creative sign that muscles are contracting to achieve the birth of your baby. Once you understand this, with breathing and relaxation techniques you can work with the muscular action of the uterus and help in the progress of your labor. It is a question of mental acceptance and physical assistance.

I remember someone who came to me when she was expecting her fifth child. When I explained the muscular action of the

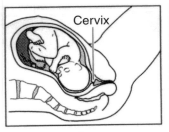

Cervix closed

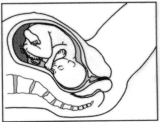

Cervix opening

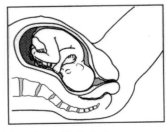

Cervix half dilated

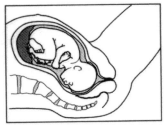

Full dilatation

uterus to her and the purpose of the contractions, she said to me, "That's fascinating. I've had four babies and I never knew the purpose of contractions before. It will make all the difference now that I know that they are doing something *positive*."

After she had had her baby, she told me, "I can't tell you how different this labor was from all the others. I went into labor with a totally different attitude. I knew every contraction was taking me that one step closer to the birth of my baby. It wasn't easy and it certainly wasn't painless, but it was something *I was doing* rather than something that was being done to me." It is this kind of positive attitude that is the most important thing of all.

Labor is Part of Pregnancy

Try not to think of labor as an event completely *separated* from pregnancy. Too often a woman thinks of it with fear and trepidation as a dark cloud that she has to get through at the end of nine months. Yet labor should be thought of as a *continuation* of pregnancy, the pregnancy that has brought various inevitable changes, both physical and emotional, that you have dealt with *as they occurred.* Labor is the final change. And, as you found during pregnancy, you will be able to deal with it as it progresses through its different stages.

Thinking about labor as another aspect of pregnancy and not as something completely separate helps to bring a more rational viewpoint to the whole process. It will also reduce some of the fears and anxieties that so often arise as the expected delivery date draws near.

During the last few weeks, a series of hormone changes are occurring that in time will start labor. There is a saying: "Pregnancy lasts for eight months and one year." Those last weeks seem to drag on forever. It is so important, during the last weeks, to keep busy, but without getting overtired.

One day at a time

Try to live one day at a time. We are all apt to look ahead, cross off dates on the calendar, look for signs and symptoms that may indicate the start of labor and then, when nothing happens, we become impatient and frustrated. I have known women who have put a ring around the estimated date of delivery on the calendar, and then refused to make any plans for the days following. If you do this, each day will seem like an eternity. So plan ahead to meet with friends, go to a movie, go out to eat or take a vacation.

This is especially important if you go past your due date, which isn't unusual. If or when your labor starts, it's not difficult to cancel arrangements. Anyone would understand if you say, "Sorry, I'm starting labor. I have to cancel our plans." The worst thing you can do is to sit at home watching and waiting. But I must stress: Don't overdo, don't keep so busy that you become exhausted. I'll say it again: **It is vital that you go into labor with a positive energy account.** Fatigue lowers the pain threshold and makes it more difficult to relax and keep on top of the breathing techniques.

50

During the last weeks of pregnancy, Braxton-Hicks contractions may become more noticeable, especially if you get too tired. These painless uterine contractions start around the 16th week, but most women aren't aware of them until the last two or three months. You may feel your abdomen becoming very tight and hard for a short time, before returning to its normal state. During second and subsequent pregnancies they may be even more noticeable. They are nothing to worry about. If they seem to change character, become regular and stronger, then it is smart to ask for advice. Labor could be starting.

There are three ways labor can start:

+ with contractions
+ with a "bloody show"
+ with the rupture of the membranes (breaking of the waters)

1. Contractions

Contractions are labor. They are a sign that the uterus is "at work." The muscles are contracting and doing the job of thinning and dilating the cervix. It is only during contractions that you are truly in labor. Too often a woman may say "I was in labor for 18 hours" or "My labor lasted 24 hours." In reality, during the first 6 or 10 hours, contractions were mild, lasting 15 or 20 seconds, and coming perhaps every 20 minutes or irregularly. If you add up the frequency and duration of the contractions, you would find that the woman concerned had been truly *in labor* for a much shorter period.

"What do contractions feel like?" is something every woman wants to know. I wish I could tell you. Everyone feels them differently. It depends a lot on the baby's position. Most women compare them to a period pain that is mild in the earlier part of labor and increases as labor progresses. For some, they start in the abdomen and radiate around to the back. Some women are aware of contractions *only* in the back. They start as an aching pain across the lower part of the back, which gradually increases in intensity as labor progresses. This can be disconcerting if you have not been warned of the possibility. I have known women who hadn't been warned who could not believe that they were in labor. Surely the contractions should be felt across the abdomen, so what is happening? I will explain the reason when I describe the different positions in which a baby may lie.

If your labor starts with the contractions, always remember that the *character* of the contractions is important—the strength and the length of time they last. You may be told that in the beginning they will come every 20 minutes, then every 15 minutes, every 10 minutes, getting closer together all the time, and that this is what to watch for. But the *interval* between contractions is not the most important thing; it is the *character* of the contraction. Some women have contractions every 10 minutes for several hours, but they are mild, lasting only 10 or 15 seconds. These contractions don't achieve very much, and it is important not to become involved too soon. If you do, your sense of time will get all out of proportion. This can only lead to a sense of impatience and frustration, which never does anyone any good.

2. The "bloody show"

During the last month or six weeks of pregnancy, you may notice your vaginal discharge increases and becomes more mucus-like. This is normal and nothing to be concerned about. It's a sign that changes are occurring; the tissues are softening in preparation for labor. As you get close to your EDD, this mucus discharge may become even heavier and streaked with a little blood. This is nothing to worry about. It does *not* mean you are about to have the baby!

There is a mucus plug in the cervix and the increased discharge is a sign that it is coming out. It's as though the uterus were saying, "I'm thinking of going into labor soon." It's a good idea to wear a sanitary pad. If you do lose blood and it soaks into the pad, it is essential to inform the hospital, doctor or midwife who is looking after you so it can be checked.

Very often if you have this "show" and are close to your date, it will only be a matter of hours before contractions start. But sometimes several days can elapse before labor proper has begun. If you have a slight show as an initial indication that labor may be close to beginning, it is vital that you do not become tense and start watching and waiting and feeling for contractions. If you are having a home delivery, it is wise to let your midwife know. If you are going into the hospital, make sure all your preparations are made and then keep yourself occupied with jobs that won't tire you. Rest. If it is the evening, go to bed early in case labor starts during the night. **Remember—it's very important for you to go into labor with your energy account positive.**

3. Rupture of the membranes — breaking of the waters

If your membranes rupture, get in touch with whoever is responsible for your medical care. They will want to see you, either in the hospital or at their office. This doesn't mean there is anything abnormal happening or to be worried about. It is just good obstetrical care. They want to make sure that the baby is well and in a good position.

The waters may just trickle out or may gush out with a "whoosh." If the latter event occurs, there is no mistake about what has happened. But sometimes the waters can trickle so gradually it is hard to decide whether it is the amniotic fluid (as the water is known medically) or a watery discharge. If you are not sure, wear a sanitary pad. If it is the waters gradually breaking, the pad will become very wet. If it is a watery discharge, the pad will be a bit sticky but will remain comparatively dry.

One other tip: During the last two weeks of pregnancy, it's a good idea to protect your mattress by putting a couple of bath towels under the mattress cover or bottom sheet. The water is colorless but might leave a stain on the satin finish of a mattress. Don't use anything waterproof, such as a plastic sheet. That is much too hot and can be uncomfortable.

Perhaps it is turning over or sitting up to get out of bed that causes the pressure that results in the membranes rupturing. I don't know. But it is interesting to note how often this happens during the night.

Mental images help

Even though the "show" or the rupture of the membranes may be your first indication that labor is imminent, it is the contractions that are the sign that labor has truly begun. So how are you going to deal with them? I'll give you some mental images to think about. They may sound childish and silly, but hundreds and hundreds of women have told me how helpful it was to have something simple to picture in one's mind.

Think of labor as a road going up a mountain and think of the contractions as steps on the road of labor, which you have to walk one by one. And remember: You can only walk one step at a time and you will never walk the same one twice. It is when we look ahead and wonder "How much longer?" that we can begin to feel negative and despondent. If you have practiced concentrating on one job at a time in your everyday life, you will find that it pays great dividends as you apply that approach to labor.

Contractions are waves. They never start suddenly, like a cramp. They start, build up to a peak, stay at that peak for a certain length of time and then gradually fade away. Usually at the beginning of labor the contractions are mild, last for perhaps 10 or 15 seconds and any pain is negligible. Remember, the interval between is not the important factor. The *character* of the contraction is the important thing. Its strength and the length of time it lasts indicate how effective it is in dilating the cervix. The mild, short ones aren't achieving much. The long, strong ones really help achieve the goal of full dilation. Until that goal is reached, it isn't possible for the baby to be delivered vaginally. Think about this. **The longer and stronger the contraction is, the *better* it is from the point of view of what it is achieving.**

As labor progresses, the waves become higher, the contractions become stronger, last longer, and get closer together until, just before full dilation of the cervix (the end of the first stage), they can come every two minutes and last nearly two minutes. In fact there is very little time between them.

'Never again!'

This is nearly always the most difficult part of labor, both physically and emotionally. Any pain is at its maximum. This is the point in labor when you may feel you'd just like to go home, forget about having a baby and make a firm decision that you will never, *never* have another one! Language can get out of control and words you would ordinarily never use may be shouted at anyone near you, especially those who are nearest and dearest.

One woman I taught many years ago shouted at her husband at this point, "I just want to go home. I know you wanted four children. Well, you'll only have one. I will never have another one." I had warned the expectant father of the possibility of this reaction during what we call the "transition stage" and because of this he laughed. Well! That made matters worse. She shouted at him, "It's fine for you to laugh. You're not having to do it." He reminded her, "Remember what Betty said. If you're feeling like this, you're almost there. Come on . . . just one at a time. Soon you'll be at the top of the mountain." She told me that reminding her of this made all the difference and helped restore that positive attitude, which is so important.

Breathing Techniques

The breathing technique that can be so helpful during the first stage of labor is simple. There are just two ways to practice.

1. Breathe gently and not too deeply, accenting the outbound breath. Breathe with your lips separated. I'm not suggesting that you breathe with your mouth open. Just let your lips be separated and then breathe out and let your breath come in naturally. It will probably come in through your nose and mouth. That's not important. What's important is that you not breathe out too deeply, then close your mouth and breathe in deeply through your nose.

2. The second way is "huffing and puffing." It sounds strange, but it can be a tremendous help during labor. It is two shallow breaths, OUT-IN, OUT-IN; then BLOW-IN, BLOW-IN. This is always done through your mouth.

It is important to practice breathing this way so that it becomes easy and natural to do. But please remember never to do it too long: no more than four breaths at the first lower, slower level, and never more than three or four patterns of huffing and puffing: OUT-IN, OUT-IN; BLOW-IN, BLOW-IN being one pattern. If you do it for too long, you could become dizzy. Once you are in labor and have a specific reason for doing it, that is, dealing with a contraction, the situation will enable you to do it as long as you need to.

So, how are you going to apply the breathing and relaxation techniques to contractions? As a contraction is starting, it is as though your uterus is saying, "I'm going to work." It goes to work, so you go to work. First, look at it with the attitude that says, "Good. I know what I'm doing. I'm going with it." It *is* good. You will have waited nine months for this baby and without contractions, the cervix will not dilate; until the cervix is dilated, the baby cannot be born. It is when there are no contractions, or they are few and far between, that you can feel frustrated and impatient.

The surfing technique

The next thing to do is this. Stop whatever you may be doing, focus your attention on some object across from you and *breathe* at that object with the idea of breathing above and away from the contraction.

Here is another simple, seemingly childish picture to have in one's mind: Imagine yourself getting on to a surfboard and riding your wave with your breathing. So many women have told me how helpful this idea has been, although one told me after her labor, "I'm kind of afraid of water and I can't swim. I felt too vulnerable, so I got myself a helicopter, jumped in, closed the door, and then I was safe!"

When the contractions are not very strong—usually the case in the early stages of labor—the breathing is at the lower, slower rhythm. It's all you'll need. As the contractions become stronger and last longer, breathing usually becomes a little quicker and shallower. But your breathing will change automatically, provided you breathe in the way I have suggested, with your lips separated and with that gentle accent on the outward breath.

"Huffing and puffing" is helpful when the contractions are becoming much stronger and you find that the lower, slower breathing is not enough to keep you above the wave. It introduces variation into the breathing and gives you more to concentrate on.

Total concentration important

It is the total concentration of your attention and breathing onto an object away from you that is so important. This is why you must **never let anyone or anything interfere with your concentration.** Warn the person who will be with you that you will not be replying. You don't need to be polite to anyone. If someone speaks to you, don't answer. Keep breathing to the end of the contraction and then you can say, "I'm sorry, I was busy." At the end of the contraction take two or three deep breaths, then relax as much as you can to recharge your energy for dealing with the next one.

Remember to breathe easily and slowly for as long as possible. Never put unnecessary effort into it. It will only make you tired and could cause you to hyperventilate and make you dizzy. I repeat—it is your mental concentration and positive attitude that is all-important.

A simple test will help you understand the purpose of your concentration on breathing. Ask someone to pinch you on the wrist. The first time, tense up against it and see how it feels. It will probably be quite painful. Now let it be done in the same way a second time. This time, drop your shoulders, and think, "Good, I know what I'm doing, I'm going with it." Then fix your attention onto some object away from you—an ornament, a picture, a spot on the wall—anything will do.

Then breathe at the object using the slower way of breathing, concentrating totally on whatever you are breathing at, and don't try to analyze what is happening at wrist level. I think that you will find the pain is very much less. I always did this to one of the 14 or 16 expectant mothers in my class to demonstrate the purpose of the breathing. Invariably she would say, "You weren't doing it as hard the second time." What favor would I do anyone if I cheated? To prove the point, I'd ask the other members of the class to do it to each other. They were always amazed at the difference concentration and breathing made, and it helped them understand their purpose.

This kind of breathing can be used in any situation that may be painful or unpleasant. I have taught hundreds of women who overcame their fear of medical shots by using this technique. Relax, accept the situation, focus your attention on something away from you and breathe.

I remember someone I taught who was terrified of getting a shot. When I suggested to her that she use this technique, she said, "Oh no, I couldn't. I hate shots. I always have. I always will. I'm really neurotic about them." "If you think so determinedly that you can't," I told her, "then of course you won't ever be able to. You are completely negative in your thinking. But if you think, 'I *might* be able to. At least I can give it a try,' and you practice it, I think you'll be surprised at what changes you can make in your attitude." And I added, "If you don't want to do it for yourself, at least try to do it for the sake of your children."

Because the fact is, we often pass our own phobias and anxieties on to our children. She was very good. She decided to try a new, more positive approach to this phobia of hers and in due course she was able to handle having shots without putting herself into a state of near panic. She laughed when she told me, "I always tell them, 'You have to wait until I've dropped my shoulders, relaxed and found my spot to breathe at.'" Overcoming her phobia made all the difference to her life. She felt far more confident and able to cope with any difficulties that arose.

The breathing-relaxation technique is not only for contractions; it's also helpful during labor if you have an internal examination. This is done to ascertain the degree of dilation of the cervix. If you tense up during an examination, it can be quite painful. Never be afraid to ask the midwife or doctor to give you a moment or two first to relax and find your spot to breathe at. It will be that much easier for you as well as for the person carrying out the examination.

And practice this technique as you go through your pregnancy when you have to confront a situation which may be painful or unpleasant. It will help build your confidence that it *does* work, that with practice it can become an automatic response to these situations—and that will be a weapon to carry with you throughout your life.

I don't suggest for a moment that the breathing and relaxation techniques make labor painless. It would be very wrong and cruel to suggest to anyone that they will. What they do is *lessen the pain.* And, very important, they will give you the feeling you can rise above it with something positive to *do,* rather than be swallowed up by it with a sense of helplessness.

And so you walk your road of labor step by step, trying not to look ahead but dealing with each "step" or contraction as it occurs. It's a good idea to keep yourself busy (but not too busy) for as long as possible. Walking is helpful. By being upright during a contraction, the force of gravity will help the baby move down. Leaning against a wall or drooping over the back of a chair can be comforting and relaxing. The time will come when you no longer want to be moving around but will feel more comfortable in bed. Never force yourself to stay active if you begin to feel tired. Fatigue only lessens the pain threshold, so rest and recharge your energy.

As you climb towards the summit of your mountain, the contractions become stronger, last longer and usually the interval between will lessen to a point where there is very little space between them. This transition stage, as the cervix is almost fully dilated, is nearly always the most difficult part of labor. Any pain is at its maximum, we feel we cannot go on much longer, and the whole business of having a baby no longer holds much joy for us. This is when you will need all your self-control and patience. As one young woman said to me, "You have to be determined through this part. I felt at one time as though it were overwhelming me, but I thought to myself, 'Each contraction for itself . . . and remember, the difficult part is nearly over.'"

No situation in life is ever all good or all bad. There are always two sides to every coin—the positive and the negative. The more we can practice looking for the positive aspect of any situation in our everyday living, the more we can build this positive attitude in ourselves. It is not easy to do and I speak from personal experience. It is only through constant practice that I have been able to change from being a rather negative, anxious person into a much more relaxed and positive human being.

Let me stress again the importance of this in labor. As the contractions become much stronger, yes, they are more difficult to cope with. But they are also much *better* from the point of view of what they are achieving. **Only the long, strong contractions are going to bring the cervix to full dilation.**

As the cervix reaches full dilation, you will begin to feel pressure on the anus, a feeling of wanting to push just as when the bowels need to move. This is a moment for rejoicing. It means that the second stage of labor, the actual delivery of the baby, is in sight, and the beginning of the second stage usually brings a tremendous sense of relief and satisfaction.

The irresistible urge to bear down is caused by the baby's head pushing through the open cervix, pressing on the anus, the opening through which the bowels move, and giving exactly the same sensation as when bowels do have to move. It is almost as if the baby is saying, "Mom, the door's wide open. It's time to push me out!" It is important to understand the reason for this sensation, because otherwise it can be very embarrassing.

I remember a woman who, many years ago, came to me for her second baby, when expectant mothers were less well-informed, telling me that with her first baby she suddenly felt her bowels were going to move. She ran to the toilet and started to push! Luckily a midwife appeared very quickly and got her back to bed, where the baby was born soon after. "I couldn't believe it," she told me. "It felt exactly as if he was coming out from the wrong place."

Sometimes there is a delay from the moment when you want to push and the time when you are allowed to do so. This is because the cervix has not dilated symmetrically. The front has pulled up more quickly than the back, allowing the baby's head to press down on the anus through a cervix that is not quite fully open. This is called an *anterior lip*. You may hear a healthcare provider saying, "There's just a lip left"—a little disconcerting if you don't know what it means!

If this occurs, you will be asked *not* to push. It's important that you do not actively push until the cervix is fully dilated.

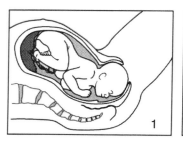
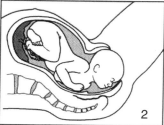

1–2 Progress of the second stage

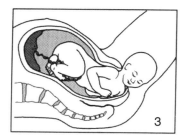
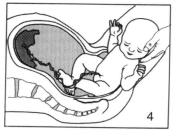

3–4 Delivery completed

Sometimes it can be difficult not to push, but huffing and puffing can come to your rescue. To push, you have to hold your breath, and by continuing with the breathing you will be able to prevent yourself from giving in to this urge. You will feel the pushing sensation. Nothing can stop that, but by preventing yourself from actively pushing with the contraction you will help the cervix fully dilate. The golden rule is if you aren't sure, do not push. A doctor or midwife will tell you when the cervix is fully dilated, which means that magic moment has arrived when you are about to start the job of pushing your baby out into the world.

One word of warning

During the first stage of labor, some women experience uncontrollable bouts of shaking and shivering. Without previous warning, this is very alarming. If it occurs, never try to stop it. Trying only increases it. Although it won't be easy, relax as much as possible and breathe slowly and deeply. Usually these attacks of shivering won't last long.

~ 7 ~

The Second and Third Stages of Labor

The start of the second stage of labor brings with it a tremendous sense of relief. Now, at last, you can do something physically active towards achieving the baby's birth. Pushing the baby down the birth canal can be hard work. It truly is labor, but for most women, if the baby is in a good position and you are pushing correctly, any pain you have experienced now disappears.

The second stage can last from just a few pushes, taking only five or ten minutes, up to a couple of hours. Not that you would be pushing without stopping for two hours; there is always a period of rest between contractions. During second and subsequent labors the second stage is nearly always accomplished much more quickly than during a first labor. In fact, it can sometimes be overwhelmingly quick.

Your position for the delivery can vary. It is wise to discuss this in advance with the professional who is going to help you. The most important factor is never to lie too flat. Many years ago women were delivered lying flat on their backs, which went against everything Nature intended. For the baby to come down the birth canal it is essential for you to be propped up at an appropriate angle. Some people advocate a squatting position. This is sensible as far as the correct angle is concerned, but for the majority of women it is impossible to maintain for any length of time.

Right position for pushing, head forward and chin tucked in.

I've found that a very comfortable position is to be propped up, preferably against a hard support with pillows. It enables you to push correctly and allows a back rest for you to relax against and recharge your energy between contractions.

How to push the right way

How do you push correctly? As a contraction starts, lift up your legs, hold your arms around your thighs, take in a big breath, hold it, tuck your chin down on your chest and push as though you were trying to make your bowels move.

Tucking your chin down towards your chest is *very* important, because it will help you push in the right direction. If you hold your chin up and your head back, you will give yourself a sore throat and achieve nothing toward getting your baby delivered.

Another important point is to let your legs fall apart as much as possible and not to squeeze your buttocks together. This will allow the muscles of the pelvic floor to relax. Sometimes women feel a stretching sensation as the baby is moving down, and tighten up against it. Try to resist this temptation. The best way to do this is to let your legs fall apart.

I have known women who have been a little frightened by the idea of pushing a baby down the birth canal, because they imagined that the baby's head is hard. One young woman said to me, "That's what I dread. I lie awake sometimes and think of pushing something large and round and hard down that small passage, and it makes me feel sick." **A baby's head is not hard—it is soft and has the wonderful capacity for molding itself to the shape of the birth canal.** The birth canal has an amazing capacity for stretching. This same woman had a very happy labor and told me afterwards that the second stage had been one of the most exciting experiences of her life.

Push longer, not harder

The secret is to push *long*. Sometimes you will hear people say "push harder," but it should never be harder, it should always be *longer*. It is the continued pressure downward, toward your rectum, that will help move the baby down the birth canal. When you stop pushing, the baby will move back a little, and at the end of the contraction the baby will also move back. But don't despair! At the beginning of the next contraction the baby's head will return to the point it had reached at the end of the last contraction, and then you'll be able to push it a little farther down the birth canal. Knowing this, you can see that if you are giving a series of short, hard pushes, you won't be achieving very much.

When you have pushed as long as you feel you can, let your breath go, quickly take in another, and push again. You'll be able to do three or four long pushes during most contractions. Don't waste time between pushes. Think of holding the baby down and not letting him or her slip back. Many women can feel the baby moving down. Go with this feeling. Get the idea of pushing your baby *out*, not of holding him or her in. You will know when the contraction is over, because the urge to bear down disappears. Lie back, relax, take a few deep breaths and recharge for the effort of the next contraction.

The moment someone says "I can see your baby's head" is an exciting one. Dark hair; fair hair; no hair: It doesn't matter! That wondrous moment of birth will not be long delayed. Pushing the baby's head around the "corner" is the hard work. Once that's achieved, the baby won't move back, and on the next contraction or two the baby's head will be "crowned" and then delivered.

This is the moment when you will be asked to *stop pushing* and to pant in and out instead. This allows the baby's head to be delivered slowly and gently. We don't want babies to pop out like a champagne cork! It's not good for the baby or for your pelvic floor muscles.

Once the head is delivered, the shoulders rotate so the baby is lying on one side. The midwife or doctor will then deliver the shoulders, and the rest of the body will slip out very easily. It is comforting to understand about the rotation of the shoulders. So often women have wondered, "Why is it that the delivery of the head is the difficult part? The shoulders are much wider." Once you can visualize the rotation of the shoulders and understand how a baby's body slides out on the side, the fear of having to push the width of shoulders through a comparatively small outlet will be alleviated.

I have never delivered, assisted at or been present at a birth when I have not experienced that sense of quiet excitement and awe on hearing the first cry that proclaimed the start of a new, independent and unique life.

I remember so well the first time I saw a baby born. I thought to myself: If you never believed in God, a Supreme Being, or whatever you want to call the Life Force that underlies the existence of all living things, you would have to believe in it after watching the miracle of birth.

How Your New Baby Looks

And your baby is born. It is a magical moment that can be marred if you haven't been warned about how newborn babies can appear. They can sometimes look very blue, but as soon as a baby cries and the lungs expand to take in oxygen the color will change. Sometimes, however, a baby can look rather blue and limp for the few moments it takes for this to happen. The molding of the baby's head, which I have already mentioned, can sometimes lead to it looking slightly elongated and misshapen at birth. This too can present a new mother with a moment of worry. She may think that her baby's head will be that shape permanently. But it is wonderful how soon this will disappear and the head will assume an ordinary, normal contour.

There are two other points to mention before we leave the subject of a newborn baby's possible appearance. First, the delivery of a baby is a far less messy business than many people imagine it to be. But as the cervix reaches full dilation, the "bloody show" becomes heavier, and, as the baby moves down and into the birth canal, some of this blood will adhere to the head. One woman, whom I taught for her second baby and who had not gone to any classes before her first pregnancy, was very frightened when she first saw her baby. There was blood on the head and she thought her baby had suffered some damage. She told me, "I felt cold with fear those first few moments. As soon as I was reassured, I was all right, but I'll never forget those first moments of panic. Please, Betty, always remember to warn people about this."

Second, it's not uncommon for the baby's genitals to be swollen at birth. With a boy, the scrotum can look very blue and swollen, and with a girl, the vulva can look the same. Many of the women I've taught have told me how thankful they were to have this information. Without it they would have thought the baby suffered from some abnormality.

Cutting the Umbilical Cord

Once the baby is born, the umbilical cord will be cut. This is a painless procedure. There are no nerves in the cord, and it is only through nerves that we feel pain.

Third Stage of Labor

The third stage of labor, the expulsion of the placenta (the afterbirth) follows. You might be asked to give a little push to help in the expulsion, but in most cases all you need to do is lie back and enjoy a wonderful sense of achievement and admire your baby.

Why stitches?

If you should need any stitches, which are necessary sometimes, they will be put in after the delivery of the placenta. They are inserted to repair the *perineum*, the floor of the genital canal between the vagina and the rectum (the back passage). It stretches during the second stage of labor, and the muscular tissue of which it is comprised has a remarkable capacity for stretching. Sometimes it doesn't stretch sufficiently, in which case an incision needs to be made to prevent it from tearing and to facilitate the delivery of the baby. This incision is known as an *episiotomy*. Many women dread this almost more than anything. They think of the perineum as being a very tender area and imagine that the process will be extremely painful. They flinch especially at the thought of having local anesthetic injected into that part. But the stretching of the skin creates a degree of numbness that helps minimize any discomfort there may be.

Pain relief

If there is any pain or discomfort from stitches, it will come during the first week after the birth. Sitting in a hot, but not too hot, bath can be a comfort, and an ice pack held against the perineum can give great relief. A package of frozen peas wrapped in a small towel and pressed against the stitches can work wonders. One woman I taught said to me, "I don't think I'll be able to eat frozen peas for a while, but I don't know how I would have managed without them during those few days after the baby was born!"

Forceps and Vacuum Extraction

So far we have discussed a normal vaginal delivery. But sometimes circumstances arise that require helping the baby out with forceps. Many women are very nervous about this. They imagine dangerous instruments that will squeeze the baby's head. Forceps are shaped like salad spoons. They are applied along each side of the baby's head, and the handles are locked together so it is impossible for them to tighten any farther.

Vacuum extraction is another method by which the baby can be helped out if necessary. A suction cup is attached to the baby's head and the baby is then gently drawn out. Circumstances dictate which method a doctor chooses:

1. The baby's position

We prefer a baby to present in what is called an *occipito-anterior position*, commonly referred to as *OA*. The back of the baby's head is towards the mother's abdomen, and the baby is facing the spine. This allows the head to flex during the first stage, which makes it easier for the head to descend through the pelvis and to be pushed around the "corner" for delivery. Sometimes a baby will lie in what is called an *occipito-posterior position*, referred to as *OP*, with the baby facing the abdomen. It is when a baby is lying OP that contractions are often felt across the lower part of the back.

Labor that starts and progresses slowly, with contractions being felt only in the back, is usually an indication that the baby is lying OP. In many instances, as labor progresses, the head will rotate and turn into an OA. But if OP persists, it will inevitably make for a longer labor. Very often, for all her splendid effort, a woman is unable to push her baby out on her own. My first baby was lying OP. He refused to rotate, so after a long labor and much pushing I needed the help of forceps. I remember being very grateful for that help when it arrived.

2. Fetal distress

During the second stage of labor, if the heartbeat shows signs of the baby becoming distressed, the delivery will be accelerated by helping the baby out with forceps or vacuum extraction so the baby's distress can be attended to as quickly as possible by the experts.

3. The mother's fatigue

A woman may become very tired, especially if the first stage of labor is protracted. Her energy account has been depleted to the point of being overdrawn and the effort of pushing becomes too much. No progress is being made. This is not good for the mother or her baby. These are the moments when one can say a sincere "thank you" for expert help and remember that forceps and vacuum extraction can be life-saving instruments.

Sometimes after a forceps delivery the mark of the forceps will show on the baby's face. This disappears after a few days. Vacuum extraction causes swelling on the baby's head where the cup was applied, but this recedes in a short time.

Cesarean Section (C-section)

Circumstances can arise when it will be necessary to perform a Cesarean section. For various reasons this action is sometimes decided upon before a woman starts her labor. Then it is called an *elective Cesarean,* and will usually be performed a week or ten days *before* her due date. Then there are the occasions when a Cesarean will be carried out during labor. The commonest reasons for this are if the first stage is very prolonged, the cervix is not dilating or if the baby's heartbeat shows signs of distress.

C-section hints

When you get out of bed—and you will be told to do this fairly soon after the operation—the last thing you'll feel like doing is to stand up straight. But make yourself do it. Press your hand gently over the area of the incision. This can be a great comfort. Then breathe as though you were breathing through a contraction and *make* yourself walk as straight and tall as possible. Walk, as it were, *through* the pain of walking. The first time will be very difficult, the second time not quite so difficult, and after some perseverance you will find you are moving about quite easily.

I have taught so many women who have told me how difficult it was to stand up straight and *walk,* but they made themselves do it and it paid great dividends. One woman who had to have a Cesarean was walking up and down the corridor three days after the operation and made a wonderfully quick recovery. She was told by her healthcare professional, "It is your just reward for moving around the way you've been doing." It's easy to give in to the tendency to lie in bed, move as little as possible and feel a little sorry for oneself. But this never does anyone any good at all!

The other hint is how to lessen the gas that can be a problem after any abdominal operation. I have mentioned how useful ginger can be in helping alleviate nausea and heartburn during pregnancy. It can be equally helpful after a Cesarean. If you don't like ginger, never force yourself to use it. But if you like it, it can work wonders.

Make the ginger tea as suggested on page 28 and sip it slowly. I have taught several women who underwent elective Cesarean sections. They took a small container of ginger root, already finely chopped or grated, into the hospital with them. It's usually easy to find someone on the hospital staff to make the tea for you. This tip was given to me by a Chinese woman who got it from her grandmother. I've heard of many who were skeptical about the efficacy of this strange concoction, but who were amazed at its beneficial effect. There are many "old wives' tales" that we reject to our regret, and there are many people who have indirectly blessed that dear grandmother.

If forceps, vacuum extraction or a Cesarean section become necessary for a first delivery, it doesn't mean they will be necessary for subsequent labors. I myself, having needed forceps for my first labor, delivered my second baby spontaneously after only three hours. I know many women whose babies were delivered by Cesarean section because they were lying in a breech position (that is, bottom down instead of head down), but who subsequently had normal, vaginal deliveries when the babies were presenting head down.

New mothers sometimes feel unhappy when they have needed a Cesarean or other assistance with the delivery. They feel they failed somehow. The baby didn't come out the "right way." Please remember that the most important factor is the safe delivery of a healthy baby to a happy and healthy mother.

There is no blueprint for labor. No two are ever alike, and if you have six babies you will find all your labors are a little different. That's why it's so important to go with the particular pattern of your labor as it progresses, contraction by contraction. It's true that first labors usually last longer than any other, particularly second stages, but don't take this for granted, because babies can be quite unpredictable. I'm certain of only one thing: The relaxed, confident woman who knows how to cooperate with the muscular action of her uterus will keep the length of labor to its minimum.

Inducing Labor (Induction)

Induction is the artificial starting of labor. There are several reasons why this may be required:

1. If pregnancy continues past the due date to the point at which placental activity may be diminished and therefore affect nourishment to the baby.
2. If, earlier in pregnancy, the growth of the baby slows below normal because of placental insufficiency.
3. If there is a sustained increase in blood pressure.

There are different methods of inducing labor. If it is suggested, never be afraid to ask the reason for it and how it is going to be done. It's always reassuring to know the reasons for any medical procedure that may be undertaken.

Pain Relief

There are several methods for controlling pain during labor. *Analgesics* (pain-killing drugs) can be given by mouth, injection or through inhalation. Epidural analgesia will usually eliminate pain in the lower half of the body. It is administered by introducing an analgesic drug into the epidural space that surrounds the spinal cord. It does *not go into the spinal cord.* Many women are nervous about having an epidural. They imagine a needle being inserted into the back and left there throughout labor. This isn't the case. The drug is introduced through a very fine, hair-like catheter that is securely strapped to your back. Its presence will not be noticeable to you. An epidural can sometimes make your legs feel very heavy. They become difficult to move, in which case you will need help in changing position. Having an epidural does *not* mean you have to lie still in one position, often a fear of many women whom I have taught.

Epidural analgesia can be useful in protracted labors, such as for a baby lying OP, and is frequently used during Cesarean section (C-section). Its great advantage, when used for Cesarean section, is that the mother can remain conscious for the delivery of her baby, hear the first cry, hold her baby immediately and feel that she has "been there" for the birth. A word of reassurance: A screen is held in place so the operation is not visible to the mother, or to the father, if he is present to give comfort and support and to share in the wondrous moment of his baby's birth. But no man should be made to feel guilty or a failure if he does not feel able to be present during a C-section.

I mentioned a sense of guilt or of failure. In my experience, many pregnant women set standards that they feel must be achieved during labor. I remember one woman who was determined to have no pain relief whatsoever. She was determined to do it "on her own." She said to me, as have so many others, "Oh! I don't want to have any drugs. I want to do it naturally, by myself."

This attitude can cause problems. As labor progresses, if pain increases to the point where it becomes difficult to deal with, the determination to do without help can cause physical tension, which in turn will increase pain, which will cause greater tension, and so the spiral grows. Then, if circumstances make it necessary to accept some sort of pain relief, the woman who has started labor with this rigid dislike of having any help may feel a sense of failure and be left with unhappy memories.

When I had shown my breathing technique to this woman, and explained how useful it can be in any situation that may be painful or of which one is fearful, she said, "Good. I'll use it when I go to the dentist and have to get a shot." "Do you get a shot at the dentist?" I asked her. "Oh, yes. I'm not good with pain and I hate shots." I laughed. "You'll accept help from the dentist but refuse to accept it during labor." She got the point.

I have taught thousands of women who have gone through labor and delivered their babies relying entirely on breathing and relaxation techniques. I have also taught thousands of women who have been grateful for the help analgesics can give. My advice always is to go into labor with an open mind. Remember— we can never predict what pattern a labor will follow. With confidence and understanding, walk your road of labor step by step, using the relaxation and breathing techniques you have practiced. Accept help if it becomes necessary. This positive atti- tude will keep the need for any outside help to a minimum, and the minimum amount will have the maximum effect.

Motherly Love Not Always Immediate

A few words here about your reactions when your baby is born. People speak of that ecstatic maternal love that overwhelms every mother at the moment of birth. It is just not true that every mother experiences such emotion. Many do, but many women cannot accept the reality of the baby for several weeks. They can be made to feel very guilty by the friends and relatives who are cooing over the baby, expecting them to show all the joy and excitement of new motherhood.

The idea of childbirth and motherhood as a wonderful, beau- tiful, mystical experience can be dramatized to the point where it becomes a woman's firm expectation. When the reality falls short of her expectations, she can be severely traumatized. Every woman's experience with childbirth is *different,* and no one knows how she will react to it until that time arrives.

Some mothers want to hold their babies immediately, even before the umbilical cord is cut. Others want to wait until the baby has been wrapped up before holding him or her. It doesn't mean one will be a "better" mother than the other.

Over the years I've heard from mothers who had long and dif- ficult labors. "I was so tired that I really didn't want to cuddle the baby. I was afraid I might drop him." "I was too tired to take a real interest in the baby for two days. Now I love her to death."

"Thank goodness you warned us that we aren't always overcome immediately with motherly love. Otherwise I would have felt very guilty."

Bonding

There is a lot of talk about the importance of "bonding" between mother and baby, and that this will be impaired if the mother and her baby don't have *immediate* contact. But sometimes a particular delivery necessitates putting the baby into a special-care unit, which prevents such close physical contact. I have known of many such cases, but it hasn't hindered the building of a wonderful happy relationship between the mother, her baby and her growing child. Any feeling of guilt or failure that a new mother is made to feel does more harm than the temporary separation from her baby.

One of my "mums" told me that the resident pediatrician in the hospital where she had her baby posted a notice there that said, "It can take time to fall in love with your baby." What a wise man!

Practicing

Practicing for labor is essential. By practicing I don't mean just doing the few exercises I have suggested and learning the relaxation and breathing techniques. It is practicing with your mind, with your thinking, that is so vitally important if you are to build the positive approach that will make your reactions automatic once your labor starts.

First of all, picture in your mind what is happening in your uterus during a contraction. Imagine those long muscles pulling the cervix up and one by one opening the door so your baby can be born. Think about it from time to time as you go through your day. The fact that what you imagine about the muscle action is not anatomically or physiologically correct doesn't matter.

It's important that the purpose of the contractions becomes implanted in your mind. The only way to achieve this is by thinking about it during those weeks leading up to labor. Talk to yourself about the important points I've mentioned. This may sound like the first step on the road to craziness, but I promise you it works. The critical phrases are:

+ Each contraction is taking me one step nearer the goal.
+ Never let anyone or anything interfere with my concentration during a contraction.
+ The stronger they are, the better they are.
+ There is only ONE to deal with at a time.

Occasionally practice a contraction. Say to yourself, "Here comes one," then stop whatever you may be doing, focus your attention on a spot across from you and breathe, pretending it is a real contraction. By practicing in this way it will become an automatic response by the time labor starts for real.

Someone I taught told me that one day her husband heard her talking to herself and then saw her stop, stare into the distance and start breathing. "What on earth are you doing?" he asked. "I'm practicing my contractions . . . One at a time . . . Each one is one step closer to the baby . . . The stronger they are, the better they are." Poor man. He was amused until the principle was explained to him. She told me that by practicing in this way, and by thinking about it all like this, it had become so much a part of her that once labor started, she didn't have to think about it. As a contraction started, she automatically found herself breathing and thinking, "There is just this one to deal with."

For the second stage of labor, I suggest that you do *not* practice the actual pushing. But now and then, when you are sitting in a comfortable chair, tuck your chin down and think to yourself "Press . . . push *long*." By doing this, by using the creative thinking part of you in this way, you will build these two vital points of the second stage into your mind, and they will be there for you when the time comes for you to push your baby out into the world.

For anyone who already has a child or children, it is wise to explain the breathing technique to these little ones. Even if they are too young to understand the principle of the breathing, let them see you practicing. Otherwise it could be frightening if you were to have a contraction and start concentrating on your breathing in their presence. Many of my mothers expecting second and subsequent babies have told me that their children have enjoyed practicing the breathing themselves. One small 4-year-old put a pillow under her pullover, was seen to be breathing and was heard saying, "I'm having a baby!" I have a feeling that she will be spared any negative fears of pregnancy and childbirth as she grows up.

Practicing takes very little time. Just thinking about it and stopping occasionally to act out a contraction takes no more than a few minutes during a day. But those few minutes will pay great dividends as you go through your labor.

~ 8 ~

The Postnatal Period

"It takes a year to have a baby, not nine months."
I have repeated those words to thousands of expectant mothers, urging them to have respect for those three very important months *after* their babies were born. More often than not the most difficult part of having a baby is neither pregnancy nor labor, but the time after you take your baby home. Few of my "mums" really listened or believed what I said and followed my advice.

When they returned for a few refresher classes during their next pregnancies, time and again I was told, "I wish I had listened to you and taken your advice and rested more. I couldn't believe how tired I would feel. I will never make the same mistake again." The mistake they had made was to try to go too far, too fast, too soon. It always made me sad to hear of problems that could have been avoided if only new mothers had gotten their priorities right.

Those first weeks of learning how to look after a new baby are not easy. Babies are demanding. Reality soon replaces the advertisement pictures of pink-cheeked, chubby cherubs, always smiling or sleeping peacefully. Babies cry and need feeding. Babies need bathing. Diapers need changing. Laundry has to be done. It all takes a great deal of time and effort. With time and practice your confidence in handling your baby will grow and life will become easier.

One young mother, who came to my classes before her first baby was born and returned for a few "refresher" classes in preparation for her second, asked me to tell women who were expecting first babies to remember that a baby becomes easier and easier to take care of. "I'm sure it would help mothers to know that after those first three months it gets a lot easier. During those early months it always seemed like there was so much to be done that I wondered if I'd ever have time for myself again."

Maternal Anxieties

Like all other parents, especially of first babies, you will suffer the normal anxieties over your baby's health. You will probably keep checking to make sure that he or she is all right. If the baby cries, why is the baby crying? If the baby doesn't cry, why is the baby *not* crying? My son was not a good sleeper. On one occasion he kept on sleeping like an angel. It was so unusual that I gently shook him until he woke up and cried. I wanted to make sure he was alive.

Even though I was a trained nurse who had looked after dozens of other people's babies, when I had one of my own I suffered from the same maternal anxieties as most new mothers do. It can happen to all of us. I have known many mothers who, when their babies started to sleep through the night, got up several times to check just to make sure everything was OK.

REST! REST! REST!

However trouble-free they may have been, pregnancy and labor take their toll on your energy account and leave you feeling tired. Not many babies sleep through the night for the first few months. They need to be fed, which deprives you of sleep. Added to the normal stresses and strains of looking after the baby, this inevitably leads to great physical fatigue.

The only way to counteract this fatigue is to get sufficient REST. This is the most important thing for every new mother to remember. It is essential for you to go to your bed every day for the first two weeks and REST FOR TWO HOURS. From then on, rest for at least one hour a day until your baby is two or preferably three months old. If you do this, you will never regret it. There's no excuse for not doing it, except perhaps for mothers who have other children demanding attention.

If circumstances make it difficult to take a full hour at a time, then REST for half an hour twice a day or for 20 minutes three times a day. You can always find the time if you want to. When you feel really tired, I suggest you make it a lifelong habit to take 10 or 15 minutes off to lie down, relax and restore your energy. As the years go by and your family grows up, the ability to relax completely at will for those short periods will be one of your greatest weapons for coping with the ups and downs of a busy life.

Set Your Priorities

The first priority after your baby is born is to restore your energy account and to keep it positive. Whether she likes it or not, a woman is the cornerstone of her family and her own emotions affect everyone around her. Babies react to their surroundings and the way they are handled. The more relaxed a mother is, the more contented and happy a baby will be—another vital reason for a mother not to become exhausted.

Never expect too much of yourself and overload your day with too many jobs. *Please* don't make a martyr of yourself with a compulsive idea that "this must be done" and "that must be done." The baby's needs are of prime importance and will occupy much of your day, leaving little time for the ordinary household chores of cleaning, dusting or polishing. A little dust harms no one, and your baby will be a far happier little person if he or she is looked after by a mother who is not exhausted.

Organize your day. Make a list of things to be done, and then do them ONE AT A TIME in order of importance. Realize that some jobs will have to be left undone to wait for a later date. **And always put your REST PERIOD at the *top* of your list.**

"Woman-in-the-nightgown" syndrome

Here is another suggestion many new mothers have found help-ful. Never stay in bed too late in the morning. There is the temp-tation, especially if you had a night of broken sleep, to go back to bed for more rest after feeding the baby early in the morning. It's easy then to sleep until the next feed, which might be 9:30 or 10:00 a.m. The feeding will take about an hour, bringing you to 11:00 a.m. and still in your nightgown. This is what I call "the woman-in-the-nightgown" syndrome.

Few things are more depressing than to see yourself in the mirror at that late hour of the day, looking like you did when you first got up, and knowing you have a busy day ahead of you. By the time you have washed and dressed, it is well into the day and you'll have to rush around, trying to catch up with no time to rest. By evening, you'll be exhausted.

If you go back to bed after the baby's early morning feed, set an alarm and get up no later than 7:30 a.m. Wash, dress, do your hair, put on your makeup (if you use it) and prepare for the day ahead. Think of the evening meal. If you have one, take a pre-cooked dish out of the freezer. Do whatever you can in advance—peel potatoes, wash vegetables and so on. The straw that breaks the camel's back is arriving at the end of the day, unrested, rush-ing around to get everything done and having to prepare a meal.

So get up early! Use this time, when the baby is still probably asleep before needing the next feed, to drop your shoulders, breathe, and calmly prepare for the day ahead. If you do this, you'll achieve maximum results for minimum effort. You'll have time for that all-important rest, and your new family will get off to a good start.

Visitors

BEWARE OF VISITORS! I cannot count the number of times I've heard the same story, of a day ending in tears caused by too many visitors. Of course it's good to see relatives and friends and to share with them the joy and excitement of your baby's arrival. But be careful. Visitors and continuous talking can be exhausting.

Restrict the number and length of their visits, and never let them interfere with your rest period. If you send out birth announcements, it's a good idea to add "Mother and baby rest between 1:30 p.m. and 4:00 p.m." or whatever hours you choose. It will let your friends know that you aren't to be disturbed with phone calls or visits during those hours. Many new parents who have done this have told me that it works wonders.

Here is a letter I received from one of my "mums:"

> *Stress how important it is not to have too many visitors. Friends kept coming to see me and the baby. I was so excited and proud to show him off, and I got really tired, and it affected my milk supply. The baby was hungry and crying. I was crying too, and it was just too much. In the end my husband said, "No more visitors. You're exhausted from seeing too many people." So I said "No" to anyone who wanted to come, explained why and had a very quiet week. I felt so much better after that, and breastfeeding is now going very well. I will never make the same mistake again.*

Any friend who has had a baby and remembers the postnatal period will understand why you want to limit visitors.

With all this emphasis on rest, I don't mean that you should never go out or see people. It's during the early weeks that sufficient rest is so essential. Once you've settled into a routine, I think it *is* important that you go out, see friends and enjoy yourself. I've heard stories from new mothers of feeling trapped and tyrannized by this new little being who has come into their lives. We love our babies very much, but we love them that much more when we have been away from them for a little while.

It will do you good, every now and then, to get a thoroughly reliable babysitter, dress up and have an evening out with your partner. It's easy to become so baby-oriented that the man-woman relationship is neglected. The two of you out together will help you remember that before you became parents you were lovers. For a happy, integrated family life, *all* the relationships between mother and father and baby need to be nurtured.

Postnatal Depression

A young woman who came to my classes for her second baby said to me, "I think knowing about the postnatal period is as important as knowing about labor. With my first baby, I knew nothing. No one warned me about the emotions I might feel, and I went through mental torture thinking I was abnormal."

This woman was referring to the sense of depression she had from time to time. She couldn't understand why she should feel like this and she felt guilty about it. She and her husband were very happy, they had wanted and looked forward to this baby, and now that their son had arrived safely and everything was wonderful she had bouts of feeling blue and bursting into tears.

Very few mothers escape the "maternity blues." The immediate feeling of joy and exhilaration over the birth of your baby suddenly evaporates and you find yourself bursting into tears. If it happens to you, never try to stop yourself from crying. Let the tears fall. It is partly to do with hormones and mostly to do with Nature's way of releasing tension.

Days of depression, feelings of incompetence, moments of questioning one's ability to be a "good" mother are not unusual. When those moments of doubt, depression and inadequacy strike you, the best thing to do is talk to someone about your feelings. Never keep them to yourself; they'll only grow out of proportion. If you have a friend who has recently had a baby, she will be a very good person to share your troubles with. She will have been through it all before you, and will give you the comfort of knowing that you are a perfectly normal new mother. She too went through those days of wondering whether she had been wise ever to have had a baby.

Being too tired always increases any depression. If you are sensible and rest every day, usually the bouts of feeling depressed will soon pass. If you don't rest and allow yourself to become exhausted, your problems will continue to climb out of proportion. Remember what I have said about the interaction between mind, emotion and body.

Someone I taught some years ago rang me up when her baby was about two months old. She felt depressed and inadequate. She was being neither a good mother nor a good partner, and everything was on top of her.

"Have you been resting as you should?" I asked her.

"There's no time to rest," she said, "I'm busy every minute of the day."

"There is *always* time to rest," I told her, "but you have to *take* it. Does your baby sleep during the day?"

"Yes, but not for very long. He's not a good sleeper, and when he does sleep I use that time to do the various chores I need to do."

"Get your priorities in order," I said. "Your rest is more important than having everything spick and span and meals ready on time. Dusting and ironing can wait. Your rest can't. Your problem is you are exhausted. You *must* restore your energy account. It is completely overdrawn."

I told her I would telephone her every morning to remind her to rest and every evening to make sure she had done so. She never would have lied to me and promised me that she was taking the time to have a rest every day. After three days, she was feeling better; after ten days, she felt like a different person. Her depression had lifted, she was coping with her busy life more efficiently, her baby was more contented and sleeping better. Her partner was happier and more contented as well. He called me to tell me what a difference it had made to all their lives. We don't always realize how much our own emotions can affect people around us, especially those who are nearest and dearest.

Postnatal depression and postnatal Depression

I am convinced that postnatal depression, spelled with a small "d," is due to lack of rest and the overtiredness that can result from it. There is, however, a postnatal Depression, spelled with a capital "D," which is a medical condition and needs medical attention. So if anyone, despite being wise and resting and not trying to be all things to all people, continues to feel a black cloud of depression weighing her down, it is important for her to consult her doctor. With correct attention, this is a treatable condition; if left untreated, it can cause severe problems.

Taking vitamin B after the birth of your baby can help restore energy and minimize the "maternity blues." Several B vitamins are found in various foods, but it can help to supplement the natural sources by taking a vitamin tablet that contains them all. Check with your healthcare provider first.

Hair Loss

It's not uncommon for women to experience a loss of hair following pregnancy. Handfuls of hair come out when brushed or combed. It can worry you to think you're going bald. One theory I heard from a hairdressing school is that during pregnancy normal hair loss doesn't occur. But once pregnancy is over, the loss increases to make up for it before returning to normal. Massaging the scalp with a good conditioner after shampooing may help restore the hair to its previous thickness.

Breastfeeding

It is a widely accepted fact that there is nothing better for a baby than breastfeeding, provided the woman wants to breastfeed and there are no medical reasons to the contrary. Some mothers don't want to breastfeed and circumstances make it extremely difficult or even impossible for others. Public opinion sometimes makes these women feel guilty. But guilt only causes the mother to feel tension and unhappiness, which in turn affects the baby.

I have taught women who were undecided whether or not to breastfeed. To them I always suggested, "Try. If there are any problems, you can always stop. But if you don't even try breastfeeding, you may regret it." Many of the mothers who took this advice told me afterwards how thankful they were. "I don't think I would have started if I hadn't known I could stop if I wanted to. But I love breastfeeding. I didn't think I would, but it is a special time for me and the baby." For others, problems arose and they weaned the baby onto a bottle. But they all felt that at least they had tried. They had no regrets or feeling of guilt.

For anyone wanting to breastfeed, it is important to realize that it can take time to become established. Life is easy when the baby sucks well and you have enough milk to satisfy the demands of a hungry baby. It isn't so easy when it's difficult to get the baby onto the breast to suckle. People think this happens automatically. Not always. These little people can be very stubborn.

Sore nipples and an insufficient milk supply can cause problems. There are creams and nipple shields to help with the former. The baby's sucking and emptying the breast increases the production of milk. It is also wise to remember that tizzies and tiredness can have a drastic effect on the milk supply. Always ask for professional advice and help if you have any problems with breastfeeding. Calmness and quiet perseverance more often than not overcomes any difficulties.

Whether from the breast or from the bottle, the most important thing about feeding a baby is that it should be a peaceful, happy time, both for the baby and for the person who is doing the feeding. Babies need the warm, quiet comfort of being fed in a relaxed atmosphere.

Sex after Childbirth

There is no medical reason why you should not have sexual intercourse as soon as you and your partner feel the desire for it. For some women their libido returns fairly quickly, in which case there will be no problems. But it is wise to be warned that it isn't uncommon for your sex drive to take several months to get back to normal. This can cause anxiety and tension in both you and your partner, and such tensions will only make any sexual problems worse. Knowing why you may temporarily lose your libido can help relieve the concerns you naturally feel.

Hormonal activity underlies our sexual drive. During pregnancy there are changes in the hormones and it can take time for hormonal balance to be restored.

Soreness in the perineum (area between the anus and vulva) and vagina is also a barrier to enjoyable sexual intercourse because it makes penetration painful. Massaging the perineum with vitamin E oil helps many women with this problem. I've always suggested to expectant mothers that they rub vitamin E oil into the perineum during the last two months of pregnancy. It can't do any harm, and anything that might help with postnatal perineal soreness is worth trying.

If you become exhausted, the last thing on your mind will be making love. Another good reason for having that rest!

Problems with sex

If you have any problems with sex, discuss them with your partner. Too often people keep their worries to themselves, which increases them. You may feel guilty that you aren't able to respond to lovemaking as you did before the baby was born. Your partner may feel that the baby has replaced your affection and that you don't love him as you did before. Hidden feelings like these will cause unhappiness in both of you. Talk together openly about any difficulties. Relationships are built and strengthened by sharing both troubles and joys.

If any problems with sex persist, don't hesitate to seek medical advice. There are doctors who specialize in sexual problems and you would be wise to consult one of these.

Contraception

Ask for professional advice about contraception before you resume sexual relations. Please remember that breastfeeding does NOT constitute a contraceptive. **It *is* possible to conceive while breastfeeding.** I've taught two women, each of whom had two babies in the same year—their first ones during January and the next ones in the following November and December. When they returned for a refresher class, they both said the same thing: "But Betty, I was breastfeeding, so I thought I couldn't get pregnant." This in spite of the fact that I had already explained all about contraception. So, be warned!

In Conclusion

Once you've had a baby, your life will never be the same again. Parenthood brings with it great happiness and many rewards as you watch babies grow and develop. They'll pass from one stage to another, through childhood and adolescence into adulthood, and then will fly the nest to start their own families. But along with the blessings of parenthood come the normal anxieties and responsibilities that bring their own hurdles to be surmounted. They are all part of your daily life.

Practice dropping shoulders, accepting what you cannot change, living one day at a time, doing one thing at a time. Keep your energy account on the positive side and the art of relaxation can become your way of life. It will help guide you through the difficult days and will enhance to the full all the great joys of living.

~ 9 ~

Fathers and Families

Pregnancy and childbirth are two great milestones in life. They bring great changes into the lives of men and women, both individually and as a couple. I have known many expectant fathers who felt isolated because all the attention seemed to be directed towards their pregnant partner. I have also known many expectant mothers who felt unhappy, wishing their men understood more about childbirth.

These feelings can be avoided if you both learn something about pregnancy and labor so you can share the experience as the months go by. It will help you and your partner to know that both of you understand the changes that are occurring as pregnancy progresses.

I already explained the effect that hormonal changes can have on a woman's emotions. You may be bewildered by her mood swings if you don't understand the reason for her tears, irritability or vagueness. A woman can feel guilty and unhappy about her seemingly irrational behavior. To know that you understand the reason for it, to be able to discuss with you the hopes and fears that every pregnant woman feels, and to be able to laugh together over her strange behavior relieves tension and gives her peace of mind.

It is vital that you are warned of and prepared for the fatigue she will experience after the baby is born. The first three months aren't easy. They are a period of adjustment and of building new relationships. The sheer fatigue caused by nine months of pregnancy, labor and now looking after a new baby is greater than any new mother expects. The normal anxieties over the baby's well-being, which every new mother experiences, add to the stresses and strains of these early weeks of parenthood. **It's essential that she get enough REST.**

Too many women have given themselves unnecessary problems by trying to achieve much more than they are capable of during this period. If a woman tries to go too far, too fast, too soon, everyone in the family suffers. Your help in persuading her to REST and assuring her that you understand why everything in the home is not done to perfection will be invaluable.

If you plan to be with your partner during her labor, it is essential that you understand the relaxation and breathing techniques. In chapter 6 I explain how to use it during contractions. Even if you don't plan to be there, learn the technique for your partner's sake. It will give her confidence to feel that you understand what it's all about. There are many men who aren't sure they want to be present during labor until the time comes. When they stay, they're glad they know how to give positive support and encouragement to their partner.

As well as helping your partner, it will help you to learn the relaxation techniques. Men need to learn the art of relaxation as much as pregnant women, so I hope the book will benefit you in your everyday life as well as in your role of expectant father.

Children Learn What They Live

If a child lives with criticism,
he learns to condemn.

If a child lives with security,
he learns to have faith.

If a child lives with hostility,
he learns to fight.

If a child lives with fairness,
he learns justice.

If a child lives with ridicule,
he learns to be shy.

If a child lives with praise,
he learns to appreciate.

If a child lives with shame,
he learns to feel guilty.

If a child lives with encouragement,
he learns confidence.

If a child lives with tolerance,
he learns to be patient.

If a child lives with approval,
he learns to like himself.

If a child lives with acceptance and friendship,
he learns to find love in the world.

Points to Remember—
First Stage

1. There is no blueprint for labor. Accept your own pattern.

2. Remember the Golden Rule: "Contraction, start breathing, ONE AT A TIME—I know what I'm doing."

3. Let no one and nothing interfere with your concentration. You don't have to be polite to anyone during a contraction.

4. Imagine each contraction as a wave and keep above it with your breathing. Ride your surfboard!

5. As the contractions increase in duration and intensity, let your breathing become a little shallower and quicker. BUT KEEP IT CONTROLLED AND AS SLOW AS THE CONTRACTION WILL ALLOW. DON'T BREATHE TOO QUICKLY TOO SOON.

6. Remember: The stronger the contraction, the *better* it is. It is the long, strong contractions that achieve full dilation of the cervix.

7. At the end of the first stage, when the contractions are very strong, try to ride them with a lighter, shallower breathing or use the huffing-and-puffing technique.

8. If you feel that you want to go home, that you won't have any more babies, and that you can't go on much longer, remember: You don't have to! It's a sign that the end is in sight.

9. If you want to push before you are allowed to do so, use the huffing-and-puffing technique. It will prevent you from pushing.

10. Remember: There is only one contraction for you to deal with—the one you are having *now*. Think of contractions as steps on the road of labor and walk them *one by one*. And remember, each step puts you one step closer to your goal.

Points to Remember—
Second Stage

1. Make sure that you are propped up!

2. Keep your shoulders rounded and your chin tucked in.

3. "Press push:" LONG—DOWN AND OUT

4. Relax your pelvic floor as much as possible.

5. If you are told not to push, pant.

6. Remember you aren't being compared to anyone else. There is no such thing as failure in labor.

7. Go with your own pattern as best you can, contraction by contraction. Each one is taking you one step closer to your goal.

8. Have the help of a painkiller or an epidural if and when you need it. Don't try to be big and brave. There's no virtue in it.

9. Remember: *This is something you are doing,* not something that is being done to you.

These points are repeated on the next two pages.
Cut out the pages and keep them where you can see them
throughout your pregnancy to remind you . . .

Points to Remember—
First Stage

1. There is no blueprint for labor. Accept your own pattern.

2. Remember the Golden Rule: "Contraction, start breathing, ONE AT A TIME—I know what I'm doing."

3. Let no one and nothing interfere with your concentration. You don't have to be polite to anyone during a contraction.

4. Imagine each contraction as a wave and keep above it with your breathing. Ride your surfboard!

5. As the contractions increase in duration and intensity, let your breathing become a little shallower and quicker. BUT KEEP IT CONTROLLED AND AS SLOW AS THE CONTRACTION WILL ALLOW. DON'T BREATHE TOO QUICKLY TOO SOON.

6. Remember: The stronger the contraction, the *better* it is. It is the long, strong contractions that achieve full dilation of the cervix.

7. At the end of the first stage, when the contractions are very strong, try to ride them with a lighter, shallower breathing or use the huffing-and-puffing technique.

8. If you feel that you want to go home, that you won't have any more babies, and that you can't go on much longer, remember: You don't have to! It's a sign that the end is in sight.

9. If you want to push before you are allowed to do so, use the huffing-and-puffing technique. It will prevent you from pushing.

10. Remember: There is only one contraction for you to deal with—the one you are having *now*. Think of contractions as steps on the road of labor and walk them *one by one*. And remember, each step puts you one step closer to your goal.

From *Preparing for Childbirth*, ©1997 Betty Parsons. Fisher Books, Tucson, Arizona.

Points to Remember—
Second Stage

1. Make sure that you are propped up!

2. Keep your shoulders rounded and your chin tucked in.

3. "Press push:" LONG—DOWN AND OUT

4. Relax your pelvic floor as much as possible.

5. If you are told not to push, pant.

6. Remember you aren't being compared to anyone else. There is no such thing as failure in labor.

7. Go with your own pattern as best you can, contraction by contraction. Each one is taking you one step closer to your goal.

8. Have the help of a painkiller or an epidural if and when you need it. Don't try to be big and brave. There's no virtue in it.

9. Remember: *This is something you are doing,* not something that is being done to you.

From *Preparing for Childbirth,* ©1997 Betty Parsons. Fisher Books, Tucson, Arizona.

Index

Other Helpful Books

FISHER
er
BOOKS.

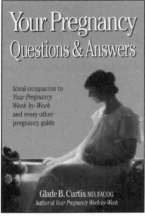

$12.95 US pb • 1-55561-068-4
$16.95 Canada, 6 x 9.25, 432 pgs,
40 illustrations
Glade B. Curtis, MD, FACOG

This best-selling guide to
pregnancy has been improved
for a new generation of babies
and mothers.

$12.95 US pb • 1-55561-088-9
$17.95 Canada, 6 x 9.25, 384 pgs,
illustrated
Glade B. Curtis, MD, FACOG

The latest in this best-selling
series—an important resource
for the many women becom-
ing pregnant after age 30.

$12.95 US pb • 1-55561-077-3
$16.95 Canada, 6 x 9.25, 448 pgs,
illustrated
Glade B. Curtis, MD, FACOG

This best-seller is easy to read
and thoughtfully answers over
1,200 questions pregnant
women ask most often.

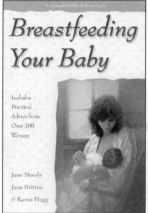

$9.95 US pb • 1-55561-114-1
$13.95 Canada, 7 x 10, 128 pgs,
fully illustrated in two colors
Margaret Martin, M.P.H.

A conception-to-birth guide
to pregnancy—written clearly
so it is extremely easy to
understand.

$12.95 US pb • 1-55561-122-2
$17.95 Canada, 6 x 9, 234 pgs
Jane Moody, Jane Britten
and Karen Hogg

Reassuring, comprehensive
advice on a subject of
increasing interest to a new
generation of mothers.

$12.95 US pb • 1-55561-061-7
$15.95 Canada, 6 x 9, 436 pgs,
40 illus., 2nd printing
Glade B. Curtis, MD, FACOG

Our best-selling *Your
Pregnancy Week-by-Week* is
now available in this Spanish-
language edition.

Available at your bookstore